ONE
Dharma

ONE
Dharma

THE EMERGING WESTERN BUDDHISM

JOSEPH GOLDSTEIN

HarperOne
An Imprint of HarperCollins*Publishers*

HarperOne

Permission and credits appear on page 212 and are a continuation of this copyright page.

FIRST HARPERCOLLINS PAPERBACK EDITION PUBLISHED IN 2003

Designed by Kris Tobiassen

Library of Congress Cataloging-in-Publication Data

Goldstein, Joseph
    One dharma : the emerging Western Buddhism / Joseph Goldstein.
        p.   cm.
    Includes bibliographical references and index.
    ISBN: 978–0–06–251701–2
        1. Buddhism—Doctrines. 2. Buddhism—United States—History—
20th century. I. Title.
BQ4165 .G65 2002
194.3'9—dc21   2001051732

        12 13 14 15   RRD(H)   10   9   8

Dedicated to all my teachers—

Those who gave me many years of guidance
And those who offered transforming moments of inspiration

In gratitude for the great blessings of the Dharma

Lord Buddha Shakyamuni, Guru Rinpoche,
Anagarika Sri Munindra, Sri S. N. Goenka,
Mrs. Nani Bala Barua (Dipa Ma), Joshu Sasaki Roshi,
His Holiness the Dalai Lama, the Venerable Mahasi Sayadaw,
the Venerable Sayadaw U Pandita,
His Holiness the Sixteenth Karmapa,
Dilgo Khyentse Rinpoche,
Tulku Urgyen Rinpoche, Nyoshul Khen Rinpoche,
and Tsoknyi Rinpoche

CONTENTS

PREFACE
by His Holiness the Dalai Lama

BUDDHISM HAS EVOLVED DIFFERENTLY IN DIFFERENT TIMES and places and yet the essential Dharma remains the same. The Buddha's prime concern was that all beings should find peace and freedom from suffering. His advice that we should try to help each other if we can and at least avoid doing one another harm remains relevant everywhere, reaching across the boundaries of nationality, language, religion and culture.

At the heart of the Buddha's teaching lies the idea that the potential for awakening and perfection is present in every human being and that it is a matter of personal effort to realise that potential. The Buddha proclaimed that each individual is a master of his or her own destiny, highlighting the ability that each person holds to achieve enlightenment. In fulfilling this aim what we need is compassion and concern for others and not self-centredness. Whether you are a Buddhist or not, these are qualities that are worth cultivating.

In recent decades improved travel and communications facilities have made our world smaller. This has at the same time made it possible for many people in the West to become more aware of Buddhism. As a result we have seen a flowering of Buddhist traditions in new lands that has not only enabled students to discover different modes of practice, but also allowed

Buddhist teachers themselves to get to know one another and share their experiences. As a young man in Tibet I myself had only very vague ideas of how the Dharma was practised elsewhere. In my long years as a refugee I have been fortunate to meet many other Buddhists. This has helped me greatly to improve my understanding of their traditions, while deepening my appreciation of other religious faiths too. I have found that extending our understanding of each other's spiritual practices and traditions can be an enriching experience, because to do so increases our opportunities for mutual respect. Often we encounter things in another tradition that helps us better appreciate something in our own.

Joseph Goldstein has been a Dharma student and teacher for much of his adult life and is a founding member of the Insight Meditation Society. He is an example of a new kind of Buddhist that we find in the West these days. Rather than holding tightly to a single tradition, he has studied with an array of teachers, integrating aspects of several Buddhist lineages into his practice. There are historical precedents for such an approach. Buddhism has often been reinvigorated when a new synthesis has been created from existing traditions. Buddhist training, wherever it has evolved, consists of certain fundamental elements such as the practices of mindfulness, loving-kindness, compassion, non-attachment and wisdom. These common themes are what Joseph has focused on here in this aptly entitled book, *One Dharma*.

THE DALAI LAMA
MARCH 6, 2002

INTRODUCTION

Sometime in the early 1970s, two Buddhist masters met in Cambridge, Massachusetts. One of them, Kalu Rinpoche, was a renowned Tibetan meditation master who had spent many years in solitary retreat in the remote mountain caves of Tibet. The other was Seung Sahn, a Korean Zen master who had recently come to the United States and was supporting himself by working in a Providence, Rhode Island, Laundromat, slowly planting the seeds of Zen in the minds of those coming to wash their clothes. At this now famous meeting of enlightened minds, Seung Sahn held up an orange and, in classic Zen dharma combat fashion, demanded, "What is this?"

Kalu Rinpoche just looked at him, wonderingly.

Again Master Seung Sahn asked, "What is this?"

Finally, Rinpoche turned to his translator and asked, "Don't they have oranges in Korea?"

We are living in remarkable times. A genuine Western Buddhism is now taking birth. Its defining characteristic is neither an elaborate philosophical system nor an attachment to any particular sectarian viewpoint. Rather, it is a simple pragmatism that harkens back to the Buddha himself, who pointedly questioned the established tenets of ancient Indian thought. It is an allegiance to a very simple question: "What works?" What works to free the mind from suffering? What works to engender a heart of compassion? What works to awaken?

In the West, our open, diverse society acts like a magnet for different spiritual traditions, and over the past few decades many people have been turning to the wisdom of the East in search of practical and tested methods of spiritual inquiry. Because Buddhist practices rely on wise investigation rather than belief and dogma, they resonate strongly with the scientific and psychological paradigms that inform our culture.

What makes this time unique in the development of Buddhism is not only that East is meeting West, but also that isolated Asian traditions are now meeting for the first time in centuries, and they are doing so here in the West. Emerging from the fertile interaction of these ancient teachings is what we can now begin to call Western Buddhism.

Not bound by Asian cultural constraints and strengthened by a society that encourages investigation, we are willing to take what is useful and beneficial from different traditions and add it to our own practice experience. These diverse methods of cultivating wisdom and compassion enhance one another and, at the same time, challenge our familiar ways of understanding. Teachings are being tested by other points of view, not in schools of abstract philosophy, but in our own lives and meditation practices. Many of us are learning and practicing several of these different disciplines simultaneously. It is not unusual for people to list as their different teachers Tibetan Rinpoches, Burmese Sayadaws, Korean, Japanese, or Chinese Zen masters, Thai Ajahns, and Western teachers of all the various schools.

This abundance and variety of teachings in one place has not happened since the great Indian Buddhist University at Nalanda, which flourished from the fifth to the twelfth centuries. According to documented reports of travelers in those times, there were over two thousand teachers and more than ten thousand monks from all over the Buddhist world who practiced and studied there side by side. Today, although we are not all gathered on one campus, the ease of travel and communication has created a similar wealth of available teachings.

But as old traditions meet in new ways, pressing questions arise. Is the melting-pot approach simply creating a big mess in which essential teachings of a tradition are lost? Or is something new emerging that will revitalize dharma practice for us all? Will it be possible to preserve the integrity of each of these distinct cultures of awakening, even as we nurture the enrichment that comes from their contact with each other? How much of our spiritual practice and discipline is embedded in cultural overlays from the East that are neither relevant nor helpful in our Western society? And do we sometimes water down—or leave behind—the essence of the teachings simply because they take us out of our Western physical or psychological comfort zone? How much can we pare away or alter before we start missing the point of it all?

Other questions too, more personal and immediate, burned in my mind as I began to study with teachers in different traditions, who often expressed contradictory viewpoints. What do you do when two of your most respected teachers say opposite things about that which is most important to you? Which fork in the road do you take when both signposts seem to point in the right direction? As I struggled with these dilemmas, one underlying and vital question began to surface: Is there a path to liberation that embraces them all?

One Dharma explores the answer to this question. It is neither a scholarly examination of comparative Buddhism nor an exhaustive study of particular traditions; rather, it is an inquiry born from my own meditation practice and from a compelling interest in understanding—and realizing—the essence of freedom.

This exploration leads to some fundamental and thorny issues: What *is* the ultimate nature of the liberated mind? Is it something already here that we need to recognize, as some of the traditions suggest? Or does it have a transcendent nature quite apart from our ordinary experience? Is it the total absence of any nature at all? Is it all of these? Do different methods of meditation practice in fact lead to different ends? Or, on the path of One Dharma, is there a way of holding even opposing perspectives in a greater unity?

The investigation of these questions requires great humility. When we step outside the safe bounds of the various individual traditions, each consistent within itself, we need to acknowledge the exploratory nature of a unified theory of Dharma, continually testing it against both our experience and the teachings as they have been passed down over thousands of years.

In Buddhism there are many names for ultimate freedom: Buddha-Nature, the Unconditioned, Dharmakaya, the Unborn, the Pure Heart, Mind Essence, Nature of Mind, Ultimate Bodhicitta, Nirvana. Various Buddhist traditions give it different names, each emphasizing certain aspects of this absolute nature. Although philosophical disputes often arise because of these different perspectives—some of these issues have been debated for thousands of years—a harmonizing understanding comes when we move away from the confines of metaphysical systems or statements and enter into the world of direct experience.

Although there are references to this philosophical discussion—and even some slight speculative indulgence—the heart of this book is practice and experience, not theory: "What works to free the mind?" I draw on aspects of three Buddhist traditions (Theravada, Tibetan, and Zen) while acknowledging that not only are there other schools of Buddhism, but even within these three, there is a great variety of lineages and sects. The criteria for reference and inclusion are simply the particular passions of my own spiritual journey: a long familiarity with Theravada teachings, the profound inspiration of a few remarkable Tibetan masters, and my great appreciation of Zen Buddhism's direct pointing to the enlightened mind.

Four basic principles, or understandings, lie at the heart of *One Dharma:* first, that philosophical concepts are only descriptions of experience, and not the experience itself; second, that mindfulness, compassion, and wisdom weave together as the essential strands of a nonsectarian path of practice; third, that what is called in Buddhism "the two truths"—the relative and ultimate perspectives of reality—together provide a framework for holding divergent points of view; and, last, that the mind of nongrasping is the essential unifying experience of freedom.

I begin, in Chapter 1, with an introduction to the meaning of One Dharma. This is followed, in Chapter 2, by a brief historical overview of early Buddhism, which highlights just a few of the issues that spawned the great profusion of different traditions. This chapter simply touches on a complex and intricate history that many scholarly books examine in great detail. It is included, though, to ground the understanding of the great movements of Buddhism in the context of their times and to draw parallels to the issues facing us today. Chapters 3–4 examine the mind-changing reflections that first bring us to the Dharma and the faith and confidence that sustain us. These are common themes in all three schools.

In the next section, Chapters 5–7 lay the foundation for the entire path of One Dharma. They are an elaboration on "the teachings of all the Buddhas," a verse from the *Dhammapada,* one of the treasured books in the Theravada tradition. Then, in Chapters 8–9, teachings from the different schools on *bodhicitta,* lovingkindness, and compassion are introduced, helping to widen the perspective of our journey. And finally, in Chapters 10–12, we see great masters from all the traditions point to the essence of the liberated mind. The temple bells of Theravada, the wooden clapper of Zen, and the long horns of Vajrayana all awaken us to ultimate freedom.

Although this outline appears very orderly, all along the way elements of the different schools weave in and out of the story. All the traditions are complete in themselves, but each one also brings a unique perspective, emphasis, and inspiration that illuminate the others in some unexpected ways. At times, Theravada discourses complement and elaborate Zen understandings. And Zen teachings sometimes resonate most deeply with profound Tibetan practices. Fundamental differences between the schools also rise up into view, and I explore the possibilities of holding them in a larger and more unified context.

My intention is twofold. First, it is to leave readers with a path of practice that integrates various teachings and methods of these several traditions—from the first steps of entering the path to the transformative experience of sudden awakening. And second, it is to show that, beneath the differences of method and philosophy, there is a deep common vein of liberating wisdom that runs through all the lineages of Buddhism. Increased mutual understanding is slowly creating the rich and subtle tapestry of One Dharma.

The implications of One Dharma for both Buddhism and our own culture are enormous. A wise cross-fertilization of spiritual practices can only deepen and broaden our understanding. It will foster not only tolerance, but also genuine respect and unity, as we each find from the great treasure-house of Dharma those teachings that benefit both ourselves and others. One Dharma is, of course, in the very beginning stages. Someone once asked an Asian teacher what Western Buddhism will be like. He replied, "We'll know in a couple of hundred years."

A FEW WORDS ARE NEEDED HERE TO EXPLAIN THE USE OF Pali and Sanskrit terms. Pali derives from the vernacular languages of Northern India at the time of the Buddha and the following few centuries (between the sixth and third centuries B.C.E.). Sanskrit was both the sacred and the literary language of ancient India. Because the Buddha believed that the Dharma should be taught in ways that even the simplest people could understand, he gave his discourses in Pali. The Theravada teachings have been preserved in this language, and this body of literature is usually referred to as the Pali canon.

As Buddhism evolved over the centuries, teachings and discourses from the later schools were written in Sanskrit, and many of the Buddhist terms we are most familiar with today are in this language. The two languages are closely related, as you can see from these pairs of Sanskrit and Pali terms: *dharma/ dhamma, sutra/sutta, bodhisattva/bodhisatta, nirvana/nibbana*. For ease of recognition, I have used the more familiar Sanskrit forms, except when quoting or referring to Pali texts. A few times you may see both forms on the same page.

ONE

MANY PATHS, ONE WAY

There is one dharma, not many.
Distinctions arise from the needs of the ignorant

—SENG-TS'AN, THIRD ZEN ANCESTOR

DAI BOSATSU MONASTERY NESTLES IN THE CATSKILL Mountains of upstate New York. About forty of us were sitting in the meditation room of the guest house overlooking Beecher Lake. It was early May, and winter was finally giving way to spring. Nyoshul Khen Rinpoche, a renowned Tibetan Dzogchen meditation master, had initiated us into the practice with empowerments, teachings, and his own amazing presence. As with many Tibetan teachers, he combined a great earthy humor with the realization of extraordinary wisdom and compassion.

The setting was tranquil and the teachings profound, yet a raging battle was taking place within my mind. There are a few times in one's life when philosophy, the love of wisdom, transforms from a gentle muse to a life-challenging god. This was one of those times. I was impaled on the sharp horns of a spiritual dilemma, and my mind could not find a way through. I felt as though I had, in good Zen fashion, swallowed a red-hot iron ball that I could neither digest nor expel.

What precipitated this crisis was the coming together of two ancient Buddhist traditions, each with its own methods, language, and philosophy, each with its own point of view. For more than twenty-five years I had been immersed in the teachings of the Theravada tradition, particularly as it was taught by the Venerable Mahasi Sayadaw of Burma. His profound wisdom and knowledge were largely responsible for the renaissance of interest in the practice of Satipatthana, also known as the "Four Foundations of Mindfulness," the practice the Buddha called the direct way to awakening. From this Burmese perspective, the practice of meditation leads to a freedom that transcends even awareness itself. Anything less than that is to still be caught on the wheel of life and death.

But in that spring of 1992 I was hearing Dzogchen teachings about the nature of mind that didn't quite fit the Burmese model. Dzogchen, also known as the "Natural Great Perfection," is the highest teaching of the Nyingma school in Tibetan Buddhism. In language both poetic and inspiring, Rinpoche was teaching the Dzogchen view that the union of awareness and emptiness *is* the very nature of the liberated mind. So for more than a month two questions plagued me mercilessly: "Which path is right—freedom transcends awareness or freedom is awareness?" and "How could I know?"

After several weeks of valiant but vain efforts at reconciliation, it became clear that I would never resolve these questions through my thinking, reasoning mind. What to do? I was benefiting tremendously from both practices and teachings, and I had deep respect for all my different teachers. Out of this intense grappling with a conflict that seemed to hold the direction of my entire spiritual life in the balance, there spontaneously arose one of those transforming moments that bring with them an unpredictable resolution. I realized that with regard to the ultimate nature and description of the fully enlightened mind, I just didn't know. A new mantra began to emerge in my practice, and it was a very truthful response to the conflicts that had been plaguing me: "Who knows?"

But instead of ignorance or confusion in this "not knowing," I felt released from the self-built prison of spiritual concepts and models I had accumulated over many years. An amazingly fresh breeze of interest and openness blew away some long-held opinions about the ultimate nature of reality. Is awareness the end of the spiritual path or is it a means to the end? Or both? What is the nature of awareness? Instead of holding to conclusions, it became more interesting and spiritually vital to hold the questions.

"Don't-know mind," a phrase often used by Zen master Seung Sahn, enabled me to embrace a variety of perspectives, seeing the different views and methods as skillful means for liberation, rather than as the statements of absolute truth I was taking them to be. It is this understanding that provides a context for exploring the One Dharma of freedom.

"Skillful means" is a phrase often found in Buddhist literature referring to the particular methods and practices used to help people free themselves from the bonds of ignorance. As skillful means we can employ whatever is useful, whatever is truly helpful. For each of us at different times, different traditions, philosophical constructs, and methods may serve us, either because of temperament, background, or capacities. For some, the language of emptiness may be as dry as the desert, while for others it may reveal the heart-essence of liberation. Some may quickly recognize the nature of awareness itself, while others emphasize the letting go of those mind states that obscure it. Some may find that the path of devotion truly empties the self, but for others this way may simply act as a cloud of self-delusion. We each need great honesty of introspection and wise guidance from teachers to find our own skillful path.

The Dalai Lama offered words very much to this point at a Buddhist–Christian conference held in 1996 at Gethsemane

Abbey, the monastery where Thomas Merton lived and wrote for many years. Buddhist monks and practitioners from many different traditions—Tibetan, Burmese, Cambodian, Sri Lankan, Chinese, Thai, and American—as well as Christian monks, nuns, and laypeople from a variety of orders expressed a wide range of viewpoints about self and soul, meditation and prayer. When the Dalai Lama spoke of his understanding at this conference, he often said, "This is right for me. Your way of understanding may be right for you."

If we hold metaphysical views (metaphysics being that branch of philosophy that examines the nature of reality) as statements of truth, conflict is inevitable, as we have seen in religious and ideological wars throughout history. And even in the more benign philosophical controversies of Buddhism, adherence to views has created sharp divisions of belief. Ideas of "right" and "wrong" are quickly followed by thoughts of "us" and "them." Attachment to our own way of understanding then becomes the primary and misplaced issue of faith. But if we think of all metaphysics as skillful means, as tools for evoking new ways of perceiving, as methods for letting go of suffering, then it's easier to open to someone else's point of view. In this way, it actually becomes possible to learn from one another.

WHAT IS ONE DHARMA?

A thousand years ago, a great monk from Nalanda University named Atisha traveled from India to Tibet to help reestablish the purity of the monastic way of life. He was sixty years old when he arrived in Tibet and, although he had planned to stay only three years, he remained there until he died at the age of seventy-two. At one point, Atisha met one of the renowned translators of Buddhist texts into Tibetan, who asked him how best to practice. Atisha replied, "You should find the essential point common to all the teachings and practice that way."

One Dharma is just this: experiencing the essential point common to all the teachings. But with so many different traditions and schools and ways of practice, how do we go about finding this common essence? Two things help us accomplish this. First, we need to create a foundation of basic understanding that will support our broader investigation. Because most of us have not grown up in a Buddhist culture where the fundamentals of Dharma are taught from childhood, we need to have some depth of experience and understanding in one practice before we can intelligently look for—and find—what is held in common by many paths. Rushing this process can simply lead to confusion.

The second means of realizing One Dharma, which applies even as we are practicing any one particular method, is an attitude of openness to diverse views and a willingness to learn from different perspectives. The great abundance of teachings now in the West offers innumerable styles of practice and systems of understanding. The result is a wealth of skillful means that allows each of us not only to find the particular method that suits our temperaments and aspirations, but also to draw on the richness and depth of many traditions. After we have become established in one tradition, we can then learn from others, understanding that at the heart of them all there is a common ground that supports our journey to freedom.

In the One Dharma of emerging Western Buddhism, *the method is mindfulness, the expression is compassion, the essence is wisdom. Mindfulness*, the method, is the key to the present. Without it, we simply stay lost in the wanderings of our minds. Mindfulness serves us in the humblest ways, keeping us connected to brushing our teeth or pouring a cup of tea. The Buddha also spoke of mindfulness as being the path to complete awakening, fulfilling our highest aspirations for happiness and peace: "This is the direct path for the purification of beings, for the surmounting of sorrow and lamentation, for the disappearance of pain and grief, for the attainment of the true way, for the realization of Nibbana."

The expression of One Dharma is *compassion*. When we are mindful in the present, compassion becomes the natural response to the suffering around us. As we open to suffering, there is a simple and spontaneous movement of the heart to help in whatever way we can. Sometimes it is in small gestures of kindness, sometimes in more courageous acts of care and concern. We can also cultivate compassion as a practice, strengthening this intuitive response within us. Nyoshul Khen Rinpoche brought this practice to life in the most simple and direct way: "I would like to pass on one little bit of advice I give to everyone. Relax. Just relax. Be nice to each other. As you go through your life, simply be kind to people. Try to help them rather than hurt them. Try to get along with them rather than fall out with them. With that, I will leave you, and with all my very best wishes."

The essence of One Dharma is *wisdom*. The perfection of wisdom is the light that illuminates our lives, revealing both the causes and the end of suffering. Through mindful attention in the moment, we see the impermanent nature of phenomena and understand the happiness of nongrasping. And through nongrasping, we experience for ourselves the innate wakefulness of the wisdom mind.

It is not enough to know this conceptually or to be satisfied with just brief glimpses of insight. One teaching of the Buddha serves as a profound reminder as we live immersed in the busyness of the world: when we practice, wisdom grows; when we don't practice, it wanes. Wisdom is not something we get and then have forever; rather, it is an understanding we need to nourish and develop in our lives. The Buddha's way is vast, and the potential for each of us is boundless. But it is up to us to take the next step.

TWO

THE EARLY HISTORY

The temple bell stops
But the sound keeps coming
Out of the flowers.

—BASHO

BEFORE WE GO FURTHER IN OUR DISCOVERY—OR REDIS-
covery—of One Dharma, it is helpful to understand its beginnings. How did the one teaching of the Buddha end up becoming
so many different paths?

Siddhartha Gautama was born a prince of the Shakya clan
in 566 B.C.E. in what is now the border region between India
and Nepal. (There is no agreement among modern scholars
about the exact date of his birth; it ranges all the way from 566
to 368 B.C.E.). Surrounded by all the luxuries of his time, he
felt a "call to destiny" that came in the form of four heavenly
messengers: an old person, a sick person, a corpse, and a wandering mendicant. Seeing them prompted the same question in
Siddhartha's mind that confronts us all. In the midst of the
great cycles of life and death, where are freedom and happiness
to be found?

At the age of twenty-nine, the prince left his palace and family in search of answers to this universal question—not philosophical answers, but transformative understandings of the heart. After six years of strenuous practices and austerities, Siddhartha sat under the Bodhi Tree in Bodh Gaya resolved that he would not get up from his seat until he had experienced for himself the deepest and most liberating truth. Through the three watches of the night he saw with increasingly refined vision his own past lives, the birth and death of beings according to their karma, and the liberating insight into how suffering in our lives is born from ignorance and ends through wisdom. Then, at the moment the morning star first appeared in the sky, his mind opened to the deathless, the unconditioned freedom that is beyond birth and death. In that moment of liberation he became the Buddha, the Awakened One, awakened from the dreamlike state of ignorance. The words that first came to him are the now famous verses that proclaimed his freedom:

I traveled through the rounds of countless births,
Seeking but not finding the builder of this house.
Sorrowful is birth again and again.
O Housebuilder, you have now been seen,
You will build no house again.
Your rafters [defilements] have been broken,
Your ridgepole [ignorance] shattered.
My mind has attained the unconditioned,
Achieved is the end of craving.

For the next forty-five years, the Buddha wandered Northern India teaching all those who wished to practice this path of freedom.

The Buddha did not teach Buddhism. He taught the Dharma, a Sanskrit word that means "the truth," "the way of things," "the natural laws of mind and body." He taught the truths of suffering and its causes, the end of suffering and its path. In eighty-four thousand discourses (a classical number used to mean "a lot") the Buddha expounded in both simple and subtle ways the profound meaning of the Dharma. His teachings were always to specific people and were geared to the temperaments and capacities of each of his listeners. Consequently, we find in the Buddha's teachings an incredible wealth of skillful means to employ in our own spiritual journeys.

During his lifetime, the Buddha also laid down rules that established and organized the community of monks and nuns, the Sangha, which preserved it as a monastic order, in various forms, for more than twenty-five hundred years. Although the monks requested that he appoint a successor at the time of his death, the Buddha refused, saying that the teachings and the monastic discipline together would serve as the most reliable guide for future generations. This one decision had striking implications. It has kept Buddhism relatively free of any centralized hierarchical structure and allowed a profusion of traditions to flourish under the umbrella of the great Bodhi Tree of awakening.

This metaphor is brought to life, even today, in Bodh Gaya, where Sri Lankan and Thai monks in their saffron robes circumambulate the tree; where red-robed Tibetan monks and nuns do their hundred thousand prostrations, recite mantras of compassion, and light thousands of butter lamps when important teachings are given; where East Asian priests of different lineages make offerings to the Buddha and sit silently in meditation; and where Westerners schooled in each of these traditions carry on their respective practices. There is one tree, but it has many branches.

To understand the emergence, richness, and diversity of these traditions, it is necessary to clarify three important terms: *Buddha*, *arhant*, and *bodhisattva*. How these terms have been understood over the centuries has played a key role in the history of Buddhism. A *Buddha* is one who has attained perfect and complete awakening, having uprooted all the defilements of mind, such as greed, hatred, and ignorance. A Buddha has completely eradicated all the obscuring tendencies and veils in the mind and is endowed with the perfection of wisdom and all-pervading compassion. These perfections express themselves through ten powers unique to the Buddha, which enable him to employ countless skillful means to help liberate beings. In the vast expanses of time in the Buddhist cosmology, many Buddhas have appeared. Siddhartha Gautama is the last historical Buddha of our age.

An *arhant* is someone who is likewise fully liberated, having freed his or her mind from all the mental afflictions that cause suffering. The classic declaration of such an attainment is called the lion's roar: "Birth is destroyed, the holy life has been lived, what had to be done has been done, there is no more coming to any state of being." Although the liberation of mind is complete, arhants do not possess the ten special powers of the Buddha or the same depth and range of wisdom and compassion.

Bodhisattvas are those who, out of great compassion for the suffering of beings, aspire to become fully enlightened Buddhas. In order to accomplish this, they postpone their final awakening until all the qualities of Buddhahood have been perfected. All schools recognize the power and purity of the bodhisattva path. It was the path Siddhartha himself followed over countless lifetimes. But the question of whether it is a path for just a few exceptional individuals or a way that many can follow became one of the great dividing issues in the historical unfolding of Buddhism.

THE FIRST COUNCIL: PRESERVING THE LEGACY

The Buddha died at the age of eighty, and in the following centuries several great councils of monks were held to review and codify his teachings, sometimes in harmony, sometimes in strong contention. According to tradition, the First Council happened soon after the Buddha's death, when five hundred arhants came together to standardize the teachings and the monastic rules.

Ananda, the Buddha's attendant and younger cousin, recited the discourses of the Buddha, beginning each one with the words, "Thus have I heard." The Pali texts that remain with us today all open with that phrase, reminding us of the great oral tradition of those times. Aside from just a few minor points about the rules, there was general assent at the First Council to the accuracy of the recitation.

Although there was agreement about what the Buddha taught, still, over the years, different schools of theory and practice began to emerge, each with its own emphasis and interpretation. Because these teachings were passed down in an oral tradition, different groups specialized in memorizing one part of the teachings or another. For example, some monks or nuns devoted themselves to reciting the Vinaya, the monastic rules. Others preserved different discourses of the Buddha, called the Sutras. Still other groups focused on memorizing the seminal teachings of the Abhidharma, the detailed and subtle Buddhist psychology. Naturally, each group gave primacy to its own emphasis.

In addition, the monks had spread over all of Northern India, and later over the whole subcontinent, often with great distances and poor communication separating them. Without the overriding authority of the Buddha himself, it was inevitable that monks and nuns in each region would develop and practice in their own way. Communities formed around particular teachers, each emphasizing their own particular understanding of the Buddha's words. There is a Tibetan saying, "Every valley has a different language, and every teacher has a different Dharma." From the very beginning, there was an ethos of pragmatism, of adapting methods to the particular needs and circumstances of the individual. The Buddha himself was the great exemplar of this, and it continues to this day, even within the most orthodox traditions.

One contemporary example of this is in the teachings of Mahasi Sayadaw. Recognized as one of the great meditation masters and scholars of the twentieth century, he was so highly regarded that he held a leading role in the most recent Sixth Council. No one seriously questions his orthodox credentials, yet he was largely responsible for two major changes in Burmese Buddhism.

The first was the inclusion of the laity in dedicated meditation practice. Although many laypeople practiced—and became enlightened—in the time of the Buddha, over the centuries intensive spiritual practice largely became the domain of the monastic order. It was Mahasi Sayadaw who first opened hundreds of branch monasteries and centers where laypeople could come and practice meditation. Realization was no longer the exclusive domain of the monks, and the benefits of this expansion have played a major role in the emergence of Western Buddhism.

The second change involved methods of practice. Traditionally, mindfulness of breathing entailed the awareness of the breath moving in and out at the nostrils. A well-known discourse of the Buddha, the *Anapanasati Sutta,* explains the method in detail. Yet the Venerable Sayadaw found that people sometimes became attached to the concentration and stillness produced by this method. He then taught another way of practicing, that is, watching the rise and fall of the abdomen as the breath goes in and out of the body. For many, this created a better balance in the mind, leading onward to deeper insights.

It would seem that this was a harmless enough change. Yet when "rise and fall" was first introduced, it created a firestorm of dispute among some of the traditional monks. Although there was basis for it in the Buddha's discourses, it did not have the same historical weight as the older method. The intensity of the debate may seem reminiscent of the arguments in *Gulliver's Travels* over which side of the egg to crack open, but it points to one of the larger issues going back to even the earliest years after the Buddha: how to preserve the integrity of the teachings and, at the same time, allow and encourage adaptation of methods to current needs.

THE SECOND COUNCIL: HARBINGERS OF CHANGE

As interpretations of the teachings diversified, strong controversies began to arise over the rules for monks, over doctrinal points, and over the very meaning of Buddhahood. In the *Parinibbana Sutta*, an account of the last days before he died, the Buddha told Ananda that the minor rules of the monastic order could be abolished. Unfortunately, Ananda never asked which of the rules were the minor ones, and so disputes later arose over whether any of them could be changed.

In 386 B.C.E., a hundred years after the Buddha's passing away, a second council was called to resolve some of these disagreements. Monks from the Eastern city of Vaisali had proposed ten exceptions to the rules and raised five points of controversy regarding arhants. In addition, they considered whether monks could follow the practices of their personal teacher even if they were not found explicitly in the texts. These proposals planted the seeds for the great divergence of traditions that would soon take place.

The Eastern monks declared that, although arhants are enlightened and therefore free of impurities, because they are not fully perfected Buddhas and do not have the full range of the Buddha's mind, some subtle veils of ignorance must still remain within them. Given this alleged limitation, these Eastern monks were unwilling to give ultimate authority to the council of arhants. They wanted a more inclusive decision-making process to decide the authenticity of what could be considered the Buddha's teaching, even if it meant no longer relying exclusively on the established texts. It is interesting to note that these monks came from the Vajjian republic, the most democratic of the ancient North Indian city-states. Similar to many in the West today, they were not culturally inclined to easily accept authority.

The more orthodox elders, many of whom were arhants themselves, did not approve. They honored the greater power of the

Buddha's mind, but held that the liberation of the arhant was complete and free of any obscuring defilements. They felt they were preserving the authentic teachings of the Buddha both as they had been passed down and in their own experience of liberation. The majority of Eastern monks then broke away, calling together their own council of both arhants and nonarhants, and created a separate school called the Mahasanghika, or "Great Assembly."

What brings to life this perhaps otherwise dry history is the underlying critical issue raised at the Second Council, over twenty-four hundred years ago. It is a question that still confronts us today, confronts not only every spiritual tradition, but also each one of us on our own journey: Who or what constitutes ultimate spiritual authority? Is it a person at the top of a religious hierarchy or one's own teacher? Is it the remembered words of the spiritual founder? Is it a democratic group process that decides what is true? Or is it left to each individual? These are not easy questions, and we find them alive and well in contemporary Buddhist communities.

From one side, we understand that, although wisdom is equally available to anyone who undertakes its cultivation, not everyone is equally wise. The Buddha often advised us to associate with the wise and to avoid fools if we wish to deepen our own understanding. It makes sense to defer to those who are more enlightened than we are as we walk on the spiritual path. In this context, the discipline of awakening is not a democratic process. In a monastery or retreat center we don't vote on the hour of the wake-up bell or the meditation instructions given in interviews. We rely on the wisdom of the teacher. This is no different in principle from seeking out the most accomplished surgeon or the most skilled mechanic.

From the other side, though, we may have difficulty accurately assessing a person's wisdom. Especially in the West, where Buddhas and arhants seem to be few and far between, there is usually some mixture of wisdom and ignorance in those who are teaching. Someone may have profound insight in some areas and be immature in others. And even a quite enlightened being does not necessarily know how to run an organization. So there may be some value in relying on the group wisdom as well.

Returning to those Buddhist monks in ancient India, the fundamental issue was not just about whether particular rules should be preserved or abandoned. The more important question was whether the Buddha's words as remembered and compiled in the recitations (and later in the written texts) were the only reliable authority for ascertaining the truth of a teaching or whether there was the possibility of transmission outside of the texts, based on one's own understanding and realization. The great movements of Buddhism find their roots in one side or the other of this debate.

The Theravada (Pali for "Teachings of the Elders") tradition, now found in Sri Lanka, Burma, Thailand, Laos, and Cambodia, is the heir of those more conservative monks who chose to uphold all the rules and preserve the tenets of the original oral teachings. They preserve the arhant ideal as the difficult but accessible culmination of the spiritual path. They took the Buddha's words to heart when he said let the teachings and the rules be your guide in the future.

The breakaway monks of the Great Assembly were the precursors of what slowly evolved into the schools of the Mahayana (Pali and Sanskrit for "Great Vehicle") and, later, Tibetan Vajrayana (Sanskrit for "Diamond Vehicle") traditions. They generally espoused a more liberal interpretation of the rules and a less orthodox interpretation of the original teachings. By lowering the status of the arhant, they began the gradual introduction of the bodhisattva as a universal spiritual paradigm and not just a path for a few unusual beings. This shift begins to change the emphasis from the Buddha as an exceptional, but historical, human being to the Buddhas and Bodhisattvas as archetypal figures who transcend time and history.

From their first beginnings in India after the Second Council, the Mahayana schools later spread to China, Tibet, Korea,

Japan, and Vietnam. The emphasis in Zen practice on enlight-enment as a direct mind-to-mind transmission outside the Sutras harkens back to that early discussion. And the vast panoply of Buddhas and Bodhisattvas in the Tibetan tradition likewise finds its first roots in this historical development.

THE TURNINGS OF THE WHEEL

After his enlightenment, Buddha Shakyamuni ("Sage of the Shakyas"), spent seven weeks near the Bodhi Tree contemplat-ing various aspects of the Dharma. Wondering who would be receptive to his profound realization of awakening, he thought of the five ascetics who were his companions during his years of intense austerities. The Buddha then went to Sarnath, a small village outside of what is now Benares, where these ascetics were staying. His first teaching to them is called "Setting the Wheel of the Dharma in Motion," and it lays out the Four Noble Truths, the basic doctrine of liberation common to all Buddhist schools. These four truths are the truth of suffering, its cause, its end, and the path to that end. This teaching is the first turning of the Wheel of Dharma, a wheel of awakening that over the centuries would roll over much of Asia and eventually cross the great oceans to arrive in the West.

But as Buddhism evolved in India and different teachings emerged in the various schools, new Sutras appeared, emphasiz-ing emptiness, the bodhisattva path, and intrinsic Buddha-Nature. According to these later traditions, it was the Buddha himself who elaborated these teachings, through a second and then a third turning of the Wheel of Dharma. He did this not in his ordinary physical body, but in the visionary and mystical manifestations of his enlightenment.

The framework of these three turnings of the Wheel of Dharma has itself become a source of disagreement between tra-ditions. Theravadans generally dismiss the notion that the teachings "evolved" from the ones the historical Buddha originally taught, seeing the later discourses—and the notion of further turnings—simply as creations of the emerging philosophical schools. On the other side, Mahayana and Vajrayana practitioners view the original teachings of the first turning as being fundamental but not complete, and maintain it is only through the more mystical manifestations of Buddhahood that we come to a full understanding of reality.

In his book *The Diamond Sutra,* Mu Soeng, a contemporary Buddhist scholar and teacher, describes the differences between Theravada and Mahayana in this way:

> I like to call the earliest layer "Psychological Buddhism," and the later phase, the so-called Mahayana, "Visionary Buddhism." These terms are not exclusive but manage to capture the basic orientation of each of the two phases. The use of the term "Psychological Buddhism" acknowledges the tremendous revolution Siddhartha Gautama brought about in the religious climate of his time, moving the debate from metaphysical speculations to the working of individual consciousness. . . .
>
> This argument sees Visionary Buddhism not as a rejection of Psychological Buddhism, but as a refocusing of elements that are strongly present in the enlightenment experience of the Buddha, though wisely not the main thrust of his teachings. For such an experience is beyond the grasp of ordinary mind.

Although we might desire to order the differentiation and growth of these traditions with precise historical benchmarks, it was, in fact, an organic and intricate unfolding that happened gradually and incrementally over centuries. We go from the One Dharma of Gautama Buddha to the proliferation of schools in the centuries following his death. Through their contact with one other, these schools absorbed elements from each other, and so it is quite impossible to speak of them as isolated streams.

There were more councils and more splits, as the organic flowering of theory and practice continued. But as the traditions

moved across Asia into different cultures, they became more isolated from one another, and many of the differences hardened
into their own traditional orthodoxies, often with sectarian
overtones.

Today we are coming full circle and there is again a great
cross-fertilization across traditions. The factors nourishing the
emergence of One Dharma at this time are the great wealth of
teachings readily available and the dilemma of assessing diverse
points of view, each true and verified from its own perspective.
When we have learned from and respect the masters and teachings from various traditions, our challenge becomes how to hold
them all in wisdom rather than in confusion or conflict.

Western Buddhism will inevitably be a synthesis of these
great wisdom traditions. It is already happening. This need not
be a watering down or a mixing up of different teachings. We
can practice each of them in its own integrity and come to a
genuine depth of understanding. But when we see them all as
skillful means for awakening, rather than as absolute statements
of truth, we stay free of the sectarian divide that has plagued so
many spiritual traditions and come to the essential points common to all of them. This can be the great gift of our culture to
the long historical sweep of the Buddha's teachings.

THREE

ENTERING THE PATH

The dharma is nobody's property. It belongs to whoever is
interested.

—TIBETAN PROVERB

ALTHOUGH THERE ARE MANY DIFFERENCES AMONG THE
various religions of the world, and among the various schools of
Buddhism itself, there is also a great deal in common, most
noticeably when we begin the journey. For almost all of us, the
first step on our spiritual path, the gateway of One Dharma, happens when we find ourselves yearning for a deeper understanding
or a sense of peace and completion away from the superficial
conventions and entanglements that often seem to engulf us.

But, we ask, how can we nurture this interest in the midst
of the busyness and cares of our everyday lives? Is there some
way to redirect our attention toward the truth, toward compassion, so that we create a context of meaning for all the many ups
and downs of our experience? Within all the traditions of
Buddhism—although articulated most systematically by the
Tibetans—there are four powerful mind-changing reflections
that, when well practiced, put us on the glide path of awakening.

They are called the *four reflections that turn the mind toward the Dharma*. These guide us through our distractions and keep us heading in the right direction.

THE FOUR REFLECTIONS

Precious Human Birth

The first of the mind-changing reflections contemplates *the preciousness of our human birth*. In the vast cosmology of the Buddha's teachings there are many planes of existence, from realms of suffering to heavens of wonderful sense delights and formless bliss. There are countless world systems, immeasurable expanses of time, and rebirths without beginning. Within this rich and infinite play of existence, taking birth as a human being is held to be a rare and precious event. It's as if we have somehow arrived at a great treasure island, where, when we know the way, all good things can be attained. In this human form we have the potential to understand the causes of happiness and the freedom to cultivate them. And there is just the right balance of difficulty and ease to motivate us to do so.

Whether or not we believe in past or future lives or in the existence of other realms, we can still practice this reflection that turns our mind toward the Dharma when we consider the circumstances of our present life situation. At this moment, we may have sufficient leisure, resources, and interest to explore a path of awakening, but all these conditions are changeable and uncertain. In so many places in the world people can be living peaceful and stable lives, and then in a moment something happens and their lives are turned upside down. Natural disasters like floods, earthquakes, and violent hurricanes occur; war or violence breaks out, or someone experiences the sudden onset of some life-threatening disease. None of us are exempt from these changing conditions.

Reflecting on the existence of favorable circumstances in our lives and remembering that they are not always present arouse energy in us to make best use of these times—times that only exist through our precious human birth. Can we see all these conditions as a gift and a blessing, rather than taking them for granted and assuming that they will always be there?

Even in unfavorable times and situations, human birth itself affords opportunities to deepen our wisdom and compassion. One of my most beloved teachers, a woman from Bengal named Dipa Ma, went through periods of enormous personal suffering. While she was living in Burma with her family, her husband and two of her three children died within a short period of time, leaving her inconsolable. She described her sorrow as bringing her to the very edge of death. After almost five years of debilitating grief, a friend brought her to a meditation center in Rangoon, and she began what became an extraordinary inner journey. The depth of her suffering became the motivation for her unwavering practice, and her attainments were remarkable even in a land known for enlightened meditation masters.

We can also practice this reflection on the preciousness of human life by contemplating one of the most basic principles of Buddhist teachings—namely, that all experiences, including life itself, do not arise by chance, but through the coming together of all the necessary causes and conditions. Water freezes when it is at a certain temperature, not just because we wish it to freeze. Likewise, the conditions for our taking human birth—whatever our present circumstances—are our own past wholesome actions. We are the heirs of our own deeds. This understanding helps us regard our own particular life story, with all its joys and difficulties, with a deep and genuine respect.

One of the legends surrounding the Buddha's enlightenment— a legend found in one form or another in many traditions—illuminates this principle clearly. It describes the moments when the powerful forces of temptation, desire, and doubt assailed the Buddha's mind as he sat under the Bodhi Tree on the eve of his enlightenment. It is said that the Buddha-to-be then reached down to touch the Earth, calling on her to bear witness to his right to be sitting there, on the Diamond Throne of Awakening. Through his own past efforts he had created the conditions that would allow liberation to occur. So even as we go through the many difficulties of life and spiritual practice, we too can touch the Earth as a symbolic reminder that our human life in itself reflects our own deep worth.

This reflection is particularly helpful in our Western culture because of widespread feelings of unworthiness and disconnectedness. During one of my stays at the meditation center in Burma, at a time when my practice seemed to be at a standstill, my teacher, Sayadaw U Pandita, told me to contemplate my *sila*, which is the Pali word for "morality." He thought that by recalling past good deeds I would raise energy and delight my mind. Of course, when I heard the instruction "Contemplate your *sila*," my first inner response was, "Did I do something wrong?"

We're not often reminded to think of the good things we've done. Left to our own devices, we more often dwell on past mistakes. But reflecting in a wise way on the great good fortune of our human birth and on the many wholesome actions that have brought us here helps create feelings of joy and confidence within us.

Impermanence

The second mind-changing reflection that wakes us from the dreamlike state of ignorance is the contemplation of *impermanence*—impermanence not merely as an intellectual understanding, but rather as a way of being that has become incorporated into our living wisdom. We all know that things change, but how many of us live and act from that place of understanding? When we truly and deeply see the truth of impermanence, our hearts and minds relax. We are less likely to hold on to things, or even our own desires, quite so desperately. As we loosen our grip on what is always changing, we necessarily let go of struggle and so we let go of suffering. We can see this clearly with our own aging bodies. If we're attached to their staying a certain way, then when they change through accident, disease, or by just getting older, we suffer. Ajahn Chaa, a wonderful teacher of the Thai forest tradition, expressed it very simply: "If you let go a little, you will have a little peace. If you let go a lot, you will have a lot of peace. If you let go completely, you will have complete peace. Your struggle in this world will have come to an end."

It's sometimes difficult to see and understand that changing conditions are not mistakes. They feel that way because we sometimes think that if we were only smart enough or careful enough, we could avoid all unpleasantness—that we wouldn't fall ill or have misfortune. In fact, we usually haven't done anything wrong. It's just what happens. The Buddha talked of the eight great vicissitudes of life: pleasure and pain, gain and loss, praise and blame, and fame and disrepute. These changes happen to everyone. One of the great laws of the Dharma that I find myself often rediscovering is, "If it's not one thing, it's another."

It was this reflection on impermanence that inspired the Bodhisattva (what we call the Buddha before his enlightenment) in his quest for awakening, as he sought to discover that which is unborn and undying. "Why, being myself subject to birth, do I seek what is also subject to birth? Why, being myself subject to ageing, sickness, death, sorrow . . . do I seek what is also subject to ageing, sickness, death, sorrow?" Subject to change, why do we seek what is also subject to change? Although on some level we may see and understand the futility of seeking fulfillment in things that by their nature don't last, we often still find ourselves living our lives waiting for the next hit of experience, whether it is the next vacation, the next relationship, the next meal, or even the next breath. We lean forward and so stay forever entangled in anticipation. Reflecting on and directly observing impermanence reminds us again and again that all experience is simply part of an endlessly passing show.

My first dharma teacher, Anagarika Munindra, used to ask us, "Where is the end of seeing, the end of tasting, the end of feeling?"

There is, of course, nothing wrong in these experiences—they simply do not have the ability to satisfy our deep yearning for happiness. The wonderful paradox of the spiritual path is that all of these changing phenomena as objects of our desire leave us feeling unfulfilled, while as objects of mindfulness they become the very vehicle of awakening. When we try to possess and hold on to experiences that are transitory in nature, we are left feeling finally unsatisfied. Yet when we look with mindful attention at the constantly changing nature of these same experiences, we're no longer quite so driven by the thirst of desire. By mindfulness I mean the quality of paying full attention to the moment, opening to the truth of change. So it is not a question of closing our senses and withdrawing from the world, but of opening our eye of wisdom and being free in the world.

Liberating insight arises both from a deep and clear observation of impermanence on momentary levels and from a wise consideration of what we already know. As a way of practicing this observation, the next time you take a walk, pay attention to the movements of your body and to things you see and hear and think. Notice what happens to all these experiences as you continue on your way. What happens to them? Where are they? When we look, we see everything continually disappearing and new things arising—not only each day or each hour, but in every moment. The truth of this is so ordinary that we have mostly stopped paying attention to it. By not paying attention, we miss the every-day, every-moment opportunity to see directly, and deeply, the changing nature of our lives. We miss the opportunity to practice the "letting-go mind." "If you let go a little, you will have a little peace. If you let go a lot, you will have a lot of peace. If you let go completely, you will have complete peace. Your struggles with the world will have come to an end." In addition to noticing the moment-to-moment nature of change, careful reflections on *three obvious and universal aspects of impermanence* can also jolt us out of the complacency of our deeply rooted habits and patterns.

A first aspect to consider is that *the end of birth is death*. As time passes on, our lives just get shorter and shorter. Life only runs out. But our awareness of death often seems limited to other people; it's always others who seem to be dying. We don't often consider the reality of our own death or those of people close to us. As an experiment, imagine yourself on your deathbed looking back on your life. Imagine it as realistically as you can. What are you holding on to most? What would you have wanted to accomplish in your life? What is of most value to you in those dying moments? The great secret, of course, is to ask these questions now, when we still have time to make creative and meaningful choices. As we reflect on death, this great truth of change, do we let it in? Does it frighten us? Does it inspire us?

In *The Days of Henry Thoreau*, Walter Harding writes of Thoreau's dying days. It is an amazing account of someone who understood not only the great wonder of the natural world around him, but also the complete naturalness of his own death. Harding quotes Sophia Alcott, a friend who visited Thoreau at that time:

> Henry was never affected, never reached by [his illness]. I never before saw such a manifestation of the power of spirit over matter. Very often I have heard him tell his visitors that he enjoyed existence as well as ever. He remarked to me that there was as much comfort in perfect disease as in perfect health, the mind always conforming to the condition of the body. The thought of death, he said, could not begin to trouble him. . . .
>
> One friend, as if by way of consolation, said to him, "Well, Mr. Thoreau, we must all go." Henry replied, "When I was a very little boy I learned that I must die, and I set that down, so of course I am not disappointed now. Death is as near to you as it is to me."

Harding goes on to write, "Some of his more orthodox friends and relatives tried to prepare him for death, but with little satisfaction to themselves. . . . When his Aunt Louisa asked him if he had made his peace with God, he answered, 'I did not know we had ever quarreled, Aunt.'"

A second aspect of impermanence is that *the end of accumulation is dispersion*. All the things we gather in our lives will inevitably be dispersed. Either we lose interest in them (as so often happens), or they break, or they remain in the corner of some closet until we move or die. Yet the tendency toward accumulation is very strong. Our homes somehow keep filling with stuff, to the point where cleaning out a closet can be a major source of satisfaction.

In a wonderful documentary video by Mickey Lemle on the life of Sir Laurens Van der Post, a striking contrast is made between the Bushmen of South Africa and the Europeans who filmed them. Sir Laurens, who clearly admired and loved the amazing harmony with which the Bushmen lived in the natural world, asked them how long it would take them to prepare for a journey. They replied, "About one minute." And the film showed them picking up their few implements of survival and walking off into the desert. By contrast, as the film crew prepared to leave, there was a seemingly endless loading of the jeep with all of their Western adventure paraphernalia. The suggestion here is not that we necessarily strive to live as simply as the Bushmen—although the simplicity of their lifestyle is reminiscent of the wandering monks and *sadhus* (ascetics) of Asia—but rather that we reexamine our habits and felt need to accumulate and hold on to things in the light of understanding that all we acquire will eventually be dispersed.

Why do we invest so much energy in acquisition? There may be many psychological underpinnings of this behavior, seeing it as compensatory action, even at times compulsion, for some deeper lack. But we can also understand the force behind this habit of accumulation in a simpler way, namely, the profound influence our consumer society has on our minds. It continually reinforces desires and wanting, often co-opting spiritual values to do so. A recent automobile advertisement shows a handsome young couple standing in front of a new car, surrounded by all the latest consumer delights. The caption reads, "To become one with everything you *need* one of everything."

Because we have been so conditioned by the idea that possessions bring fulfillment, in our ordinary lives we don't have many opportunities to experience the ease of relatively unencumbered living. This may explain the growing interest not only in meditation retreats of one kind or another, but also in wilderness activity. At these times we consciously choose a voluntary simplicity in our lives that illuminates a basic and transforming truth; namely, happiness is not dependent on how much we have, all advertisements notwithstanding.

Impermanence is also seen in the fact that *the end of meeting is separation*. Our meetings with each other are like mingling in a dream. Yet we often become so intensely entangled in our relationships that separation of one kind or another becomes the source of overwhelming sorrow. The Buddha gave a striking example of this when he said that in the course of countless lifetimes each one of us has shed more tears over the death of loved ones than all of the water in the great oceans. Although feelings of loss and sorrow are natural for most of us, still, the more we contemplate and accept the truth that all meetings will end in separation, the less likely we will be to drown in those waters.

We can begin to experience the difference between love and attachment, between loss and grief. Love is a generosity of the heart that simply wishes for the happiness of others; attachment is a contraction of heart, born of desire, resulting in clinging and fear of loss. Reflecting on the inevitable impermanence of our relationships reorients us toward care and lovingkindness rather than attachment, letting go rather than clinging. The understanding of impermanence guides us toward the experience of freedom, for in these moments of nongrasping we can assess and then actually taste what is truly of value in our lives.

The Law of Karma

The third reflection that turns our minds toward the Dharma is the understanding that everything we do has an effect—*all of our actions have consequences*. In the Buddha's teaching this is called the law of karma, the understanding that we are the heirs of our own actions. It is referred to as "the light of the world," because it illuminates how our lives unfold and why many things are the way they are. Understanding karma is the key to understanding happiness.

Put simply, actions bring results. We may not always have the wisdom to see or anticipate the results correctly, or we may only have a partial vision of them, but it is this common understanding that inspires us all to act. We anticipate some result from our actions, whether it is some worldly gain or greater wisdom and compassion.

The Buddha went one essential step further in clarifying this process of action and result. The possibility for our happiness, and indeed for our entire spiritual journey, rests on the clarification that what most completely determines the result of any action is the motivation behind it. Tibetan teachings express this succinctly: *everything rests on the tip of motivation.*

We can easily see how this works in the world. There is a difference, both in how we feel and in the effect on others, between actions motivated by greed or envy and those motivated by generosity or love—even when the outward action is the same. We may give someone a gift out of a genuine loving feeling, or because we want the person to like us, or because it looks good in the eyes of others. The consequences of each of these varied motivations will be very different, both in the moment and in the long run.

Given the great importance of motivation in determining the results of our actions, it becomes essential that we actually know what our motivations are. This is not easy. We need tremendous courage, honesty, and willingness to look into our own hearts.

Staying unaware, we simply play out all the habits of our conditioning. Without knowing what our motivations are we have little chance of letting go of unskillful motivations or of developing genuine wisdom. One teaching says that if we had the choice, upon coming down to breakfast one morning, between finding either a very large sum of money or someone who could accurately point out all our faults, the latter would be of much greater value to us. Such is the benefit of self-knowledge. And yet how many of us would make that choice?

For a long time in my meditation practice I felt embarrassed and ashamed when I saw unwholesome states in my own mind, states like pride or jealousy, ill will or selfishness; and instead of examining them and working free of them, I would judge myself and dig the hole I was in even deeper. Or I would feel judged and unhappy when my teachers or other people pointed out these unwholesome mind states to me. But after years of practice I've come to feel grateful when I observe these unskillful patterns arise, because now I would rather see them than not see them. It becomes another chance to unhook from these patterns, to see their essential transparency, and to let go of the burden they bring.

Padmasambhava, the great spiritual adept who brought Buddhism to Tibet, emphasized the importance of understanding karma and the power of our motivations when he said, "Though my view is as vast as the sky, my attention to the law of karma is as fine as a grain of barley flour." Our vision of the Dharma may be vast, but we need to ground it in a wise attention to our actions.

Defects of Samsara

The fourth reflection that turns our minds toward the Dharma is the reflection on the *defects of samsara*. *Samsara* is a Pali and Sanskrit word that means "perpetual wandering," or the wandering through the endless cycles of existence. According to the

Buddha's teachings, we cycle through all the realms of existence—from the highest to the lowest—until we emerge from the dream of ignorance. We're like a bee trapped in a big jar; we may buzz around from top to bottom and back up to the top, but we remain trapped as long as the lid is on.

We see this same process at work within this life as well. For one day, notice how many different worlds you create in your mind, riding the roller coaster of continually changing moods, emotions, and thoughts. You become happy when you think about your family, frustrated at work, excited about some future plans, angry at someone who's being difficult, depressed about the state of the world, calm from your meditation . . . The play of the mind goes on and on. Samsara: perpetual wandering through the rounds of existence.

In contrast to this cycle of momentary rebirths in different states, see if you can notice carefully the moment of awakening from a long thought or mood. It is like that moment of coming out of a movie theater. The movie seemed so real when we were inside, yet so illusory when we emerge. It is just the same when we emerge from the movies of our minds. What seems so real and solid from one perspective becomes truly empty and transparent from another. One Tibetan teacher said, "Do not rule over imaginary kingdoms of endlessly proliferating possibilities."

In the moment that we awaken from being lost in a thought or feeling or reaction, in that very moment we can recognize the empty, clear, skylike nature of awareness itself. In that moment of wakefulness, we get a glimpse of freedom. And instead of judging ourselves for all the times we do get lost, which happen again and again, we can delight in each moment of awakening.

THESE FOUR MIND-CHANGING REFLECTIONS—OUR PRE-cious human birth, impermanence, the law of karma, and the defects of samsaric conditioning—turn our lives toward the Dharma, toward discovering the nature of our minds. These reflections begin to break apart the clouds of confusion and help us see the truth of our lives more clearly, help us let go more completely. Without them we are carried along on the powerful current of habitual action; with them, we enter into a timeless stream of awareness. This is not an easy task, and the great Dutch philosopher Spinoza perhaps best summed it up when he wrote, "All noble things are as difficult as they are rare."

FOUR

THE AWAKENING OF FAITH

Confident faith allows blessings to enter you.
When you have no doubt, whatever you wish can be
achieved.

—PADMASAMBHAVA

IN THE SPRING OF 1962 I WAS SITTING IN A LARGE LEC-
ture hall at Columbia University listening to Polykarp Kusch, a
Nobel prize–winning physicist. The course was "Physics for
Poets," a noble effort to interest us nonscience types in the wonders of scientific imagination. One of our assignments that
semester was to write a short paper on gravity, a phenomenon
known to all but perhaps truly understood by none. I think
Kusch was hoping for some miracle of insight bursting forth from
one of the untutored, poetic minds in front of him.

My three-page effort did not contribute much to the advance-
ment of science, but in some strange way the direction of my
thoughts at that time unknowingly presaged an understanding
that would first emerge six years later in a very different part of the
world. As a college sophomore, I put forth the notion that the
gravitational pull we feel on Earth might be the effect of falling

into an empty center, and that this pull toward "emptiness" might be extrapolated to the attraction between all bodies of matter.

Although this notion of emptiness did not have any particular relevance for understanding gravity, it began to take on new meaning as I started to learn about and practice meditation. In the early years of my practice, as I sat in Bodh Gaya with my teacher, Anagarika Munindra, he would often speak of the difficulty of escaping the gravitational field of this world of sense pleasures. Our lives seem to revolve around desire for ever new experiences, even as we see them continually changing. But through deepening our understanding of the four mind-changing reflections—this precious human birth, impermanence, the law of karma, and the defects of samsara—we begin to leave our familiar orbit and fall into, relax into, be drawn into the gravitational field of the Dharma. We begin to get glimpses of the zero center of selflessness—the Buddhist meaning of emptiness—and it becomes the new force of gravity in our lives. This is the awakening of faith, the nourishing energy of all spiritual paths. Here, it is important to recognize that faith is not a choice we make, but a way of understanding.

"Faith," "devotion," and "confidence" are all translations of the Pali word *saddha*. All of these terms refer to that feeling that opens the mind and heart to what is beyond our usual ego concerns and desires; *saddha* opens us to what is greater than ourselves, to the possibility of freedom. Faith becomes both our initial inspiration to practice and explore and what sustains our continuing efforts.

At first, our interest may be inspired by a wide range of circumstances: a book we have read, a situation in our lives, or perhaps an individual, either someone we know personally or a historical figure like the Buddha or another great being. In each case, we feel or intuit certain qualities that inspire us, qualities like courage and compassion, kindness and wisdom, generosity and selflessness. Feeling those qualities in others feeds our own deepening aspirations. We may get the scent of enlightenment.

When His Holiness the Dalai Lama spoke at several sessions of the Buddhist–Christian conference at Gethsemane Abbey, simply by being in the room with him I felt aspects of his kindness, childlike ease, and humor imprint on my mind. He had been taken on a tour of the abbey and shown the various enterprises begun by the monks to support the monastery, including making cheese and fruitcakes. When the Dalai Lama spoke to the assembly of monks and guests later that evening, he recounted the tour, saying that the monks kept offering him samples of cheese when all he wanted was a piece of fruitcake. As he was telling this story, his whole body shook with laughter. "I really wanted fruitcake and they kept offering me cheese," he said again and again, laughing the whole time. There was no distress, no real disappointment—just an openness to the experience he had had; he wasn't judging the monks or himself. The arising of faith can come in many ways—sometimes just by being with a person who opens us to a new possibility, a new way of being.

The ancient Buddhist text *The Questions of King Milinda* gives a more classic illustration of how faith and confidence arise from the example of others. This text tells how people were gathered on the bank of a flooding river, standing hesitant and afraid. One person came along, wisely assessed the situation, and found a way to cross the river in safety. Others, seeing the possibility, gathered their strength and likewise crossed to the other shore. "This bank" is our life in samsara, lost in the dreamlike enchantment of the distracted mind. The "farther shore" is the mind awakened from delusion. When we see someone accomplished, it gives us confidence that we can aspire to the same. Perhaps this is what is meant by a "leap of faith." With the inspiration of faith, we leap into the unknown, pushing our own boundary of possibilities.

Faith fuels commitment. In a more contemporary context, W. H. Murray in "The Scottish Himalayan Expedition" writes of the power of this commitment:

Until one is committed, there is hesitancy, the chance to draw back, always ineffectiveness. Concerning all acts of initiative (and creation) there is one elementary truth, the ignorance of which kills countless ideas and splendid plans: that the moment one definitely commits oneself, the Providence moves too. All sorts of things occur to help one that would never otherwise have occurred. A whole stream of events issues from the decision, raising in one's favor all manner of unforeseen incidents and meetings and material assistance, which no one could have dreamed would have come his way. I have learned a deep respect for one of Goethe's couplets:

> *Whatever you can do, or dream you can, begin it.*
> *Boldness has genius, power and magic in it.*

Faith also arises from our growing awareness of suffering. Faced with distress, we may go in one of two directions. We can fall prey to bewilderment, doubt, and further confusion, or we can begin to seek a way of understanding and release. There is suffering that leads to more suffering, and suffering that leads to its end. In times of great pain, we often drown in our feelings of despair, anger, or hopelessness. But it is also possible for that suffering to awaken a profound faith in new possibilities, to provoke our intense interest and investigation. We can ask, "What is going on? How can I understand this? Who can guide me out of this suffering?"

Suffering, uncertainty, even doubt can become our call to awakening. Although we may not yet know the path, we know we're lost and we know there is some road to travel. This can become a great and irrevocable turning point in our lives. Deep, compelling faith arises when we glimpse the possibility of freedom.

GOING WITHIN

Our first experience of faith or devotion may be in or to someone or something outside of ourselves. One of the oldest recitations of faith in Buddhism is taking refuge in what is called the Triple Gem: the Buddha himself, that person who awakened under the Bodhi Tree twenty-five hundred years ago; the Dharma, the truth, the law, and the body of teachings; and the Sangha, which means, in particular, the order of monks and nuns and, more generally, the community of wise beings. "I take refuge in the Buddha, I take refuge in the Dharma, I take refuge in the Sangha."

But in their deeper meaning, these refuges always point back to our own actions and mind states. Although there may be many false starts and dead ends as we begin our journey, if our interest is sincere, we soon make a life-changing discovery: what we are seeking is within us. The writer Wei Wu Wei, an Englishman who lived in Hong Kong for many years, captured the import of this turning within when he wrote, "What we are looking for *is* what is looking." The Buddha himself urges this understanding. In the *Parinibbana Sutta*, the last discourse before his death, he says, "Be islands unto yourselves; be refuges unto yourselves; hold fast to the Dhamma as an island; hold fast to the Dhamma as a refuge; seek not for refuge in anyone except yourselves. Whosoever shall be an island unto themselves and a refuge unto themselves, it is they among the seekers of enlightenment who shall reach the heights."

In Tibetan Buddhism, another form of taking refuge also points us back to the fundamental nature of our own minds:

In the empty essence, Dharmakaya,
In the luminous nature, Samboghakaya,
And in the manifold capacity, Nirmanakaya,
I take refuge until enlightenment.

These Sanskrit words, rich in meaning, refer to the open, ultimate, empty nature of the mind, its luminous cognizing power, and its infinite capacity for response. It is this inward movement of faith and understanding—not to a self, but to the zero, selfless center of gravity—that lies at the very heart of the One Dharma of liberation. The recognition that the whole of the Dharma is to be found within our own bodies and minds changes the meaning and quality of faith for us. No longer do we look outside of ourselves for solutions. We have seen where the path lies. All we require are the skillful means that will help us walk it.

For me this first happened while I was in the Peace Corps in Thailand. I had just become interested in Buddhism and was attending a study group for Westerners at the Marble Temple in Bangkok. Fresh from the endless philosophical discussions of my college days, I was particularly outspoken in this group, so much so that several regular members, annoyed by my persistent questioning, actually stopped coming. Finally, out of what might have been some desperation, one of the monks suggested I practice meditation. At that time I didn't know anyone who had ever meditated, and in some youthful, romantic way the idea intrigued me: the exotic Far East, beautiful temples, and Buddhist monks sitting cross-legged in their saffron robes.

After receiving some simple instruction on watching the breath and gathering just the right assortment of cushions, I sat down and set my alarm clock for five minutes. Although I might have been overly cautious regarding the length of the sitting, something quite extraordinary happened, even in those first few minutes. I saw clearly that there was a way to go inside. This itself was the revelation, not any particularly strange or exciting experience. For so long I had been trying to understand myself through books and through the eyes of other people. I had been trying to make sense of all the uncertainties I was feeling, wanting to find out who was behind the rush of thoughts and emotions that I was taking to be myself, but not really knowing how to do it. Now I saw that there was a way to directly and intimately explore my own mind. This is the transformative moment when we go from an intellectual appreciation of the Dharma to the faith and confidence that awakening is possible, that we ourselves can do this.

As we continue on the path, our faith and confidence grow stronger and stronger through our own direct experience. Faith comes, then, not only from being inspired by others, but from our own inner knowing. We begin to have confidence in the moment, in the actuality of experience. We see what is there for ourselves. What is a thought, a sensation, an emotion? What is the nature of experience free from the proliferation of concepts and limited views?

An immediacy of knowing comes from simple, uncontrived awareness. In a moment of hearing is there any doubt or confusion? We are walking in the woods; there is the sound of a bird call—just hearing. We experience a strong sense of presence. This immediacy of knowing—right now—of the breath, a sound, some movement, points to the innate wakefulness of our own minds. We learn to recognize this wakefulness, become familiar with it, and trust it. Milarepa, the great eleventh-century Tibetan yogi, said, "I attain all my knowledge through observing the mind within. . . . Thus all my thoughts become the teaching of the Dharma, and apparent phenomena are all the books one needs." It is all within us; we *are* what we are looking for.

THE POSSIBILITY OF AWAKENING

As we walk on the path of awareness, we also develop faith and confidence in the larger unfolding of our life's journey, a journey not in time or space, but a journey of our own inner understanding. *We experience the growing possibilities of awakening.* We actually *are* awake more and more, and this gives us a strong sense of path, the experience of meaningful direction. The powerful combination of presence and path, of being grounded in the present moment's experience even as we navigate toward a more complete freedom, provides a significant context for understanding our lives.

Today, in the West, the idea of having goals in spiritual practice has drawn some fire. Emphasis is supposed to be on the here and now, without thought or mention of destination. Although this has been a corrective move for ambitious ego striving and the comparing, judging mind, it has also caused us to lose something of immense value. It is often the intimation of a goal that inspires ardency and passion. In *Mount Analogue*, René Daumal writes that when you are climbing a mountain, "Keep your eye fixed on the way to the top, but don't forget to look right in front of you. The last step depends on the first. Don't think you've arrived just because you see the summit. Watch your footing, be sure of the next step, but don't let that distract you from the *highest goal*. The first step depends on the last." It is precisely our vision of the summit that inspires our journey in the first place. To lose the vision, the sense of possibility, is to narrow our view and limit our endeavor.

There is no contradiction between resting in the present moment and a sense of path or goal. We see the union of these two in every ordinary activity. When you get up from your seat, where are you going? You have some objective or purpose. We can see the amazing power of intention, leading us not only to physical destinations but to karmic destinations as well, indeed, all the way to Buddhahood.

It is in the journey of understanding ourselves that the circularity of our lives takes on meaning. We wake up every morning, eat breakfast, go to work, come home, play, perhaps even meditate, eat dinner, relax a bit, go to bed, wake up . . . and around it goes. Consider the growing mass of humanity and life forms on this small planet. One small planet revolving around a medium-sized sun, in one galaxy among hundreds of billions of galaxies.

What does this immensity mean for our lives? Are our lives leading onward in any way? When our faith in the process of deepening wisdom is strong, every aspect of our lives is part of a meaningful context. In every situation, in every moment, we can ask ourselves, "Are we awake to this moment? Are we present or not? Is there suffering? What is its cause, and what is its end?" These are not theoretical questions. They are the heart of the practice, the meaning of our lives.

The quality of faith grounds us in present experience and at the same time keeps us open to the unfolding mysteries of the Dharma. It helps us to not get stuck at any place along the way. So many times in meditation practice I have thought, "Now I've got it," only to have some new insight or perspective occur afterward, often completely unexpectedly.

Here we might usefully distinguish faith from belief. Belief draws conclusions while faith flowers in openness. Once, after several months of intensive meditation practice in Bodh Gaya, as I was doing walking meditation on the roof of the Burmese monastery, suddenly the self-conscious effort to be mindful collapsed into spontaneous, effortless knowing. No *one* was doing anything. I began dancing on the roof of the building, amazed at the ever present selfless awareness. Freedom! When I next saw my teacher and excitedly told him about my newfound experience, his only comment was, "Don't recondition your mind." Without realizing it, I had already contracted into the belief that this new experience was "it." Although it didn't make me happy at the time, having this pointed out allowed the amazing unfolding process to continue. As Trungpa Rinpoche once said of the New Age EST training of Werner Erhard, with its emphasis on *getting it*—"It isn't it."

WHOLESOME QUALITIES

The heart qualities of faith, confidence, and trust are actual powers we can cultivate. In Buddhist texts they are likened to a magical gem that settles impurities in water. Faith in the possibility of awakening, confidence in the moment's experience and in the nature of awareness itself, trust in the direction of our lives—all of these settle doubt, confusion, and agitation. They create an inner environment of clarity, stillness, and beauty.

In the Buddhist psychology (called the Abhidhamma in Pali), faith and the other wholesome qualities are termed the "beautiful mind states." We can see and recognize the beauty of these states in both others and ourselves. The expression of faith takes many forms. My teacher Dipa Ma, mentioned earlier, had extraordinary attainments, a profound simplicity, and a truly all-embracing love. Just as watching the Dalai Lama laugh over the fruitcake imprinted a certain quality of selfless, childlike humor and lightness, so too watching Dipa Ma bow to the Buddha imprinted a lasting image of the timeless grace of devotion. And in that devotion, both Dipa Ma and the Buddha disappeared. It became love bowing to love, wisdom bowing to wisdom. There was no one there.

In a somewhat less sublime way, I experienced the very pragmatic benefits of faith even in the early years of my meditation practice. I was spending my days alternating sitting and walking meditation, and during times of boredom, frustration, depression, or whatever the difficulty might have been, I often reminded myself, "Just surrender to the Dharma. Your job is to simply sit and walk, sit and walk. Let the Dharma take care of the rest." This surrender to the Dharma, the faith in the practice, kept inspiring me to continue.

THE PLACE OF PRAYER

In 1992 I was giving talks at Harvard Divinity School. A woman came up to me and asked about the place of prayer in Buddhism. At that time, I did not have much experience of prayer in my practice, and even had some resistance to the idea of it, so I replied from the Theravada perspective that what might be called prayer is the chanting or recitation of the teachings themselves. In that way, it is an impersonal reminder of basic dharma truths. Given the setting, I don't think this proved to be a very satisfying response.

Prayer plays a large role, however, in Tibetan and other Buddhist traditions, and as I began doing Dzogchen practice I began to understand and appreciate its power and place. Prayer works in different ways. It can be a practice of gratitude that we cultivate. It can be the spontaneous expression of great devotion. For some people this may be devotion to the Buddhas, Bodhisattvas, and great teachers. Prayer can also be a request for blessings from these beings for our continued growth in the Dharma. As an example of this, what follows is part of a prayer composed by His Holiness the Twelfth Gyalwang Drukchen Rinpoche:

> I call on you, my teachers—regard me with compassion!
> I sincerely wish to receive your blessings.
> Please regard your child's longing desire.
> Please bless me with the resolve to attain realization.
> Please bless me to have a steady and smooth mind,
> So that for this life and those to follow,
> As a true practitioner whose heart and mind are in accord,
> The special intention to help others is spontaneously present.
> May I be able to benefit measureless beings.

Most deeply, prayer becomes a way of realizing that our own mind is inseparable from those to whom we're praying. At this level, prayer awakens us to our own deepest nature.

When I am on retreat, I begin each day with a One Dharma ritual of prayer beginning with the Three Refuges in Pali and the Tibetan version of the Refuges mentioned earlier. Then I recite a Tibetan purification mantra to help clear away obstacles and obstructions. Following this, I create what I call a Refuge Tree, visualizing my teachers all the way up to the Buddha. Thinking of each in turn, I focus on that person's unique and special qualities and the particular ways he or she touched and inspired me. Having called them all to mind, I request their blessings for the aspirations that most deeply motivate my practice. And then I end with a few Pali verses from the Sutta on lovingkindness.

Although all of this takes only ten or fifteen minutes, it has shown me the power of prayer in meditation. It is a way of aligning our thoughts and emotions with our intentions. And it strengthens the quality of faith that keeps us open to what is beyond our immediate conventional view of the world. Prayer begins on the relative level of duality—thinking of beings outside of ourselves—but it can also connect us with the ultimate nature of mind. Who is it that is praying? And to whom?

Stephen L. Carter, in his book *Civility*, describes an interview with Mother Teresa:

> An interviewer asked Mother Teresa what she says to God when she prays.
>
> "I don't say anything," she replied. "I just listen."
>
> So the interviewer asked her what God says to her.
>
> "He doesn't say anything," said Mother Teresa. "He just listens." And before the astonished interviewer could press her further, she added, "And if you don't understand that, I can't explain it to you."

DOUBT

For faith to be grounded in the reality of our experience it must also be open enough to include what the Buddhist scholar, writer, and teacher Stephen Batchelor calls "the faith to doubt." If we use faith to push doubt aside, we construct a defensive wall to keep out any unsettling questions, to keep from having to acknowledge our own fears and uncertainties. The inclusiveness of faith lets us be with whatever arises, investigating the very nature of doubt itself and whatever other difficulties arise. By embracing doubt skillfully we strengthen faith.

Doubt is the difficult mind state of perplexity. It's like being at a crossroads and not knowing which way to go. We go back and forth between alternatives and are then brought to a standstill by bewilderment and indecision. When doubt is overpowering, we can't move. It doesn't even allow us the opportunity to take a wrong turn and learn from our mistakes.

Almost all spiritual traditions speak of the difficulty of this state and how common it is at different times on our path. Doubt can take many forms. Sometimes it is doubt about ourselves, about our ability to practice and walk the path. It is the voice that says, "I can't do this. It's too difficult. Perhaps some other time." It may be doubt about our teachers when we begin seeing their faults and limitations. It may be doubt about our path: "What does sitting watching my breath (or whatever practice we are doing) have to do with anything? It's really useless."

Doubt is very seductive because it comes masquerading as wisdom. We hear these wise-sounding voices in our minds trying to figure out the dilemmas, difficulties, and paradoxes of our experience through thinking about them. But thinking can take us only so far. It's like trying to know the experience of music by reading a book about it or the tastes of a good meal by looking at the menu. We need some other way to understand the nature of doubt, so that we can address its concerns appropriately.

The first step is to recognize when the doubting mind is present and, in recognizing this, to become familiar with its various voices. If we become aware of these voices as mental tapes, simply more thoughts in the mind, we're less likely to become ensnared by their content. In that moment, we cease to give them power: "I can't do this" becomes just another thought. We can then bring wisdom to bear on the process of doubt itself, noticing how it takes us away from the direct experience of the moment.

In 1985, I was on a meditation retreat in Nepal with Sayadaw U Pandita. We were living in crowded quarters and practicing in what I considered to be less than ideal circumstances. Five of us shared a concrete floor in a room right next to the latrine. As I did the walking meditation my mind kept getting distracted with all kinds of judgments about the others and then filled with doubts about myself, all of which seemed totally justified. When I went to report on my experience to Sayadaw, he advised, "Be more mindful." At first I thought, "Well, that's a big help!" But then I decided I may as well try following his advice. I started paying much closer attention to the movements in walking, to the sensations I was feeling. Amazingly, the mind immediately quieted down; in the closeness of attention to the body, there was not much room for all the judging, doubting thoughts. And even when they started to arise, I was no longer swept away by them. Often the simplest instruction points to an essential understanding of how the mind works.

However, sometimes when we have persistent questions or doubts in our minds, intellectual clarification can be a great help. The teachings of the Buddha are wonderfully clear and pragmatic. Often he says that he teaches just one thing: suffering and its end. On one level, we can think of the Dharma as deep common sense illuminating obvious truths that might have become obscured in the confusion of our minds. At the end of many of his teachings, people would reply to the Buddha with this refrain: "Magnificent, Master Gotama. Master Gotama has made the Dhamma clear in many ways, as though he were turning upright what had been overthrown, revealing what was hidden, showing the way to one who was lost, or holding up a lamp in the dark for those with eyesight to see."

On other levels, the Buddha analyzed the truth of suffering and the truth of its end with amazing precision and subtlety. At the heart of his teaching is the principle of dependent origination: because of this, that arises; when this ceases, that also ceases. The law of dependent origination is central to understanding not only the arising of our precious human birth, but also the unfolding process of life itself, in all its pain and beauty. Faith is the link that transforms our experience of suffering into a vehicle of awakening: faith allows us to see the suffering as a necessary condition for liberation.

In the *Connected Discourses*, the Buddha describes this process:

> Just as, bhikkhus [monks], when rain pours down in thick droplets on a mountain top, the water flows down along the slope and fills the cleft, gullies, and creeks; these being full fills up the pools; these being full fills up the lakes; these being full fills up the streams; these being full fills up the rivers; and these being full fills up the great ocean; so too . . . with suffering as proximate cause, faith [comes to be]; with faith as proximate cause, gladness; with gladness as proximate cause, rapture; with rapture as proximate cause, tranquillity; with tranquillity as proximate cause, happiness; with happiness as proximate cause, concentration; with concentration as proximate cause, the knowledge and vision of things as they really are; . . . with dispassion as proximate cause, liberation . . .

We all have taken birth; we all experience suffering. When faith is born out of that suffering rather than bewilderment or despair, it sets in motion a chain of dependent arisings leading through many kinds of happiness all the way to final liberation. There are so many stories from the Buddha's time up to the present illustrating this possibility. Particularly moving are some of the stories told by the nuns practicing during the time of the Buddha that tell of their early difficulties and their ultimate enlightenment. In the *Songs of the Sisters,* one unknown nun declared her struggle and her faith: "It is 25 years since I went forth. Not even for the duration of a snap of the fingers have I obtained stilling of mind. . . . Drenched with desire for sensual pleasures, holding out my arms, crying out, I entered the vihara [monastery]." She then recounts how she heard the teachings, sat down to one side, and realized the highest goal.

The quality of faith that kept the nun practicing through twenty-five years of difficulty is onward leading for us all, even as far as Buddhahood. In one of the Suttas, the Buddha is likened to a good herdsman leading a herd of cattle across the ford of a river. First the strong bulls and mature cows cross without difficulty. Then the younger cattle and calves cross, with a little stumbling. Finally, even the newborns cross safely to the other shore, simply by following the lowing sounds of their mothers. These newborn calves represent those who simply have faith—in the awakening of the Buddha, the possibility of enlightenment; in the Dharma, the path of our own liberation; and in the Sangha, those who have realized freedom for themselves. With the awakening of faith we have the energy to ford the streams of doubt and to bring our lives into alignment with our highest aspirations.

FIVE

DOING NO HARM

Do not take lightly small misdeeds,
Believing they can do no harm:
Even a tiny spark of fire
Can set alight a mountain of hay.

—PATRUL RINPOCHE,
THE WORDS OF MY PERFECT TEACHER

HAVING DEVELOPED SOME CONFIDENCE AND FAITH IN THE
possibility of awakening, we are now faced with a very pragmatic
question, "What do I do?" The Buddha responded to this question
with incisive and disarming simplicity: "Do no harm, act for the
good, purify the mind. This is the teaching of all the Buddhas."
The last line of this verse from the *Dhammapada* points to the
timelessness of the path. There have been many Buddhas in the
past, many will come in the future, and always the teaching, the
One Dharma of liberation, remains the same. "Do no harm, act for
the good, purify the mind." The flowering of all the great traditions
of Buddhism derives from the teachings in this one simple verse.

All the Buddhist schools agree on what unskillful, harmful
actions should be avoided and have done so for thousands of

years, yet when my colleagues and I first began teaching meditation retreats in this country, we felt a little embarrassed talking
about morality. We thought people were coming to meditate and
get enlightened, not to hear lectures on right and wrong. And in
our postmodern cultural environment, isn't all morality relative
anyway?

It quickly became clear, though, that it is impossible to separate moral and ethical behavior from meditative realization. The
entire spiritual journey rests on the morality of nonharming.
This is the expression of the love and care we feel both for others
and for ourselves. Without this foundation, wisdom does not
endure. Especially in times of changing values like our own, the
importance of personal integrity and responsibility needs to be
rearticulated again and again so we do not get lost in the confusion of our own desires. Our challenge is to give this inquiry into
essential moral values a deeper meaning, to give it vitality in a
modern world, and to do so without becoming moralistic, judg-
mental, or divisive.

From the Buddhist perspective, all of the moral precepts are
rules of training, not commandments. We undertake them as a
way of training our heart, out of care for the world and ourselves,
rather than as an externally imposed set of rules. This is a critical
distinction, because it enables us to look at our lives and our
actions without guilt and crippling self-judgment and, at the
same time, to consciously take responsibility for what we do.

Everyone wants to be happy, yet often we have very little idea
of what brings about genuine happiness. No one wants to suffer,
but do we know how to give up those actions that cause suffering? It's said that what most moved the Buddha after his enlightenment was seeing people seeking happiness, yet doing the very
things that brought about suffering. There is a Tibetan prayer
that says, "May you have happiness and the causes of happiness.
May you be free of suffering and the causes of suffering." If we
wish to be happy, we need to understand the causes and conditions that bring it about; we need to align our actions with our

aspirations. This understanding is the great compassionate gift of the Buddha to each of us, because it reminds us of the law of karma, that we are the heirs of our own actions.

Ten Unwholesome Actions

What, then, are the actions to be avoided? What are the unwholesome actions that do harm to oneself and others? There are ten actions—three of body, four of speech, and three of mind—that plant the seeds of our own future suffering. Can we use this classic teaching, shared by all the Buddhist traditions, to help us awaken from the torpor of habituated action? The Buddha is urging us to be happy by not creating the causes of suffering. These teachings provide a simple reference point for reflection, not only in the abstract but, perhaps more important, in moments of actual intention. This is practice, not philosophy.

Actions of the Body

Killing or physically harming others (or ourselves) heads the list of unskillful acts. We kill one another, kill animals for livelihood or sport, or kill things because we don't like them in our space. These are acts of violence that rebound to us in the future. Even in the present moment, look to see the separation, contraction, and alienation we create when we take the life of another. Do we stop to consider the other as a living, feeling being?

Sometimes the simple injunction "Don't kill" pushes us to the edge of our comfort zone to face some complex ethical considerations. A simple example is some unwanted and potentially harmful pests in the basement. It's easy to put out poisonous bait and have the problem disappear. But in this situation are we willing to take the time and energy to explore other options? Is it possible to capture and remove rather than entice and kill? But in other circumstances, even these good intentions may not address all the issues. What about mosquitoes that carry malaria?

Do we simply say "Be happy" and take no action? Carpenter ants are eating the floor beams of our house. We can't find a way to suggest they find another woodpile. What to do? It's sometimes difficult to find a solution that does not do any harm.

What does not killing mean in terms of our diet? Questions about this arose even in the time of the Buddha. One monk, trying to create divisiveness in the early monastic order, urged the Buddha to insist that all monks be vegetarian. Although non-harming plays such a central role in the teachings, still the Buddha found the middle way between the extremes of self-indulgence and unnecessary austerity. He recognized that within certain guidelines, it was important for the monks to accept any food offered to them as they went on their alms rounds. They were not to ask that any animal be killed for their food or accept it if one had been killed especially for them. But if a family were sharing what they had cooked for themselves, then it was acceptable for the monks to receive it.

How do we apply this in our culture today, where food is neatly packaged in the market and there is not much connection with its source? Some people perceive the clear chain of events leading from slaughterhouse to hamburger and refrain from eating meat. For others, there may be overriding health concerns that require the consumption of animal products. Or, as in many native cultures, people may accept the larger cycles of birth and death in nature and act from that understanding with compassion and responsibility. There is no one right answer to this question of diet. Our task is to stay awake to our own sensibilities, to be willing to investigate different courses of action, to not hold the taking of life lightly, and with whatever we do to maintain a heart of compassion.

The second unwholesome action to avoid is *stealing*—taking that which doesn't belong to us. Besides acts of obvious theft, stealing can also be considered on subtler levels. On intensive meditation retreats we sometimes develop a heightened sensitivity to the meaning of not stealing. During one retreat I was sharing a room with a friend and happened to use some of his shampoo without asking—a very small thing in itself, especially knowing he certainly would have offered it if asked. But in some part of my mind it didn't feel quite right. In the Vinaya, the rules for Buddhist monks, it says one shouldn't take anything worth more than a few cents without it being offered. Perhaps the dollop of shampoo fell within those guidelines, but this situation also made me aware of a level of care with the possessions of others that inspired me. Of course, we also need to find the line between being impeccable and being rigid, so that we refine our understandings with a light heart. This brings us back again to the awareness of motivation, using the letter of the law to remind us of its spirit.

Sometimes we steal by not acting as well. After I finished my time in the Peace Corps, I traveled home through Nepal, taking an overnight trek from Kathmandu to Nagarkot, a place to view Mount Everest and the surrounding peaks. It was 1967, and in those years Nagarkot was still undeveloped as a tourist site. There was only a very rough shelter with a bare room full of cots for the people who hiked up. Each cot had two thin blankets on it. Once the sun went down, people went to sleep quite early, as there was no heat and the temperature dropped quickly. I was lying in bed, feeling cold and anticipating a long night ahead. Much later in the evening, some new traveler came into the room. It seems there was only one blanket on his bed, and the caretaker asked into the darkened room if anyone had an extra blanket. I realized then that there were actually three on my cot. But still feeling cold and caught in the selfish mind seeking its own comfort, I just lay there not saying anything, pretending to be asleep. Even thirty-five years later I remember the rationalization: "I didn't ask for the extra blanket. It was just there."

Other levels of larceny can be explored as well. Are we consuming much more than we actually need—even allowing for the fact that we may not be leading a renunciate lifestyle? For each of us, this part of the teaching raises the question, "What is

moderate, and what is excess?" We can use this question either
as a bludgeon of self-judgment or as a thoughtful inquiry into our
lives and the choices we make. Waking up need not be a somber
affair when we bring the delight of investigation to what we're
doing. We can fashion our lives the way an artist creates a great
work of art. Our lives are the medium through which to express
our creative wisdom.

The poet-monk Ryokan is a great example of someone who
has found the joy of contentment. He lived from 1758 to 1831,
spending much of his adult life in the high mountains of Japan,
meditating in solitude, playing with the village children as he
went begging for food, and leaving a legacy of wonderful poetry
that illuminated his day-to-day understanding. At one point
when he had been living in a small hut with just a few essential
possessions, he returned one day to find that even his few cooking utensils had been stolen. He looked about his empty room
and then wrote this haiku poem:

> The thief left it behind—
> the moon
> At the window.

I wonder how we would react if we came home one day to
find all our possessions stolen. Would we be writing, "The thief
left it behind—the moon at the window"? Probably not!
Ryokan's life points to a deeper meaning of not stealing: the happiness of being easily satisfied with the changing conditions of
one's life.

The third unskillful action, *sexual misconduct*, requires careful
consideration. Sexual energy is a tremendously powerful force in
our lives. Often it is when we're feeling the passion of desire that
we feel most alive and vibrant. And yet we all know that heedless desire can also be very destructive, to our relationships and
to ourselves. One of my favorite moments in Burmese-English
translation happened when Sayadaw U Pandita was talking

about the dangers of sensual desire. After Sayadaw spoke for some time in Burmese, the translator then relayed the teaching: "Lust cracks the brain." In many instances, that sums it up.

So we need to be mindful with this strong energy and use it skillfully. Depending on the particular context of our lives, different actions will be appropriate. For monks and nuns who follow the monastic discipline, celibacy is the standard. For laypeople, the basic guideline is the principle of nonharming, most often expressed as refraining from adultery. We need to take care that in the excitement and energy of passionate desire we don't rationalize behavior that is deceptive or dishonest. This is not a question of prudish mores. As is evident through the extensive range of sexuality described in the Vinaya, sex was alive and well and creative in ancient India. It is precisely because sexual energy was understood to be such a dynamic element of people's lives that the Buddha took care to place sexual activity in the context of the spiritual path.

But for laypeople also, times of refraining from sexual activity can offer insight, revealing much about the nature of desire. These times show us both how strong sexual desire can be in the mind and how, like everything else, it passes. The freeing insight here is that there is nothing we have to do to make desire go away. If we just sit and observe, we will see that it comes and finally goes all by itself. This understanding is a great relief, because we begin to feel less driven by the force of our desires, no longer thinking that our happiness depends on their gratification. We still enjoy the pleasures of the senses as they come, but they no longer become the cause of harmful actions.

Actions of Speech

The next group of unskillful actions revolves around speech. It's quite amazing how often we overlook this powerful influence in our lives. So much suffering in the world comes from lack of attention to the words we use. The Buddha singled out right speech as one aspect of the path to awakening, the Eightfold Path; and of the ten unwholesome actions, four involve speech. This should be a wake-up call, a bell of mindfulness ringing before we speak. But do we really make speech part of our spiritual path, or do we relegate it to some place of lesser importance in our lives? When we pay attention, we see how much our words affect our relationships with other people, condition our own minds, and lead to karmic consequences in the future. The care it takes to avoid harmful speech creates a vast playing field of mindfulness in our daily lives.

Lying is the first in this group of unskillful verbal actions. There are many kinds of false speech, from slight exaggerations and humorous untruths, to falsehoods whose purpose is self-protection or protection of others, to deliberate lies told with malicious intent, causing divisiveness and harm.

A story of a retreatant at the Insight Meditation Society reveals how easily we can fall into habits of falsehood out of embarrassment and self-protection. Late in the evening a staff person went into the big walk-in refrigerator to get some food. She found a yogi (meditator) there with his hand in a box of dates.

"Can I help you?" she asked, quite politely.

"No," he replied, "I'm just looking for the maintenance man."

Why do we lie? Is it greed, or desire for self-aggrandizement, or fear of rejection, or jealousy? Besides the obvious harm caused by dishonesty, our lying is also a great disservice to others because it diminishes their ability to trust in themselves. They may feel something is wrong with our words, yet begin to doubt their own perceptions because of our unwillingness to be truthful. When we investigate the motives behind our own speech, they illuminate so much about the deep patterns of our conditioning. This awareness then provides us the space to make wise and sometimes courageous choices.

The book *Life and Death in Shanghai* by Nien Cheng tells an inspiring story of such choices. The Red Guards in China imprisoned the author during the Cultural Revolution. She describes the terrible conditions of the prison, and how she was repeatedly tortured to get her to falsely accuse Chou En Lai, the premier of China at that time. She consistently refused to admit untruths. After several years of this ordeal, as she was being released, she was again threatened with further imprisonment if she did not sign the desired papers. And again she refused, even in the face of renewed suffering. It is an amazing story of courage, fortitude, and unswerving devotion to the truth.

In the same way, although the Bodhisattva committed many misdeeds over the countless lifetimes of his journey toward enlightenment, from the time it was predicted that he would one day become a Buddha, it is said that he never knowingly spoke what was untrue. It was this unshakable commitment to truth that kept bringing him back to the path of awakening. When truth, on all its levels, is the polestar guiding our actions, we keep probing, learning, and questioning further. It was not until he had achieved full awakening that the Bodhisattva fulfilled his quest.

In the great Buddhist understanding of life and death and rebirth, with so many planes of existence, there are some things of greater value than life itself. Many of the Jataka tales are stories of the Bodhisattva in both human and animal form sacrificing his life out of commitment to truth or compassion for others. To whatever extent we are able, can we put this commitment to truthfulness at the very center of our own training? The principle is simple, but it's surprisingly difficult to implement. It takes strong mindfulness, alertness, and courage to see ourselves honestly and to speak what is true. But it has the power to transform—and simplify—our lives.

The second kind of unwholesome speech is the use of *harsh, angry, or aggressive language*. Words have the power to harm, and we need to be conscious of the energy and motivation behind them. How do we feel when angry, carping words come at us? Probably we feel somewhat hurt, a bit defensive, and possibly aggressive in return—not the best internal environment for open communication. This is probably how other people feel when we vent angry, harsh language toward them. The intent here is not to suppress whatever feelings we may have, but to communicate in a way that fosters connection rather than divisiveness. Questions arise about what to do with feelings of anger and the rush of speech that often follows them. In later chapters we will discuss how to skillfully be with the full range of our emotions.

But as is often the case, the Buddha saw more deeply into our unskillful patterns of response and saw that the feelings arising in us have as much to do with how we listen as with what is being said:

> Bhikkhus, there are these five courses of speech that others may use when they address you: their speech may be timely or untimely, true or untrue, gentle or harsh, connected with good or with harm, or spoken with a mind of lovingkindness or with a mind of inner hate. . . . Herein, Bhikkhus, you should train yourself thus: Our minds will remain unaffected, we shall utter no unskillful words, we shall abide compassionate for their welfare, with a mind of lovingkindness. And starting with him, pervade all the world with a mind imbued with lovingkindness—abundant, exalted, immeasurable, without hostility, without ill will.

In listening, and especially when we find ourselves becoming reactive in one way or another, we can apply mindfulness to what is being said, simply recognizing the words as timely or not, true or not, and so on. This is the meaning of mindfulness. It is not agreeing or condoning, but simply acknowledging: "Yes, this is what's happening." This clear recognition and acceptance then gives our minds the opportunity to stay open, making possible an appropriate response motivated by wisdom and kindness rather than anger and ill will.

Backbiting and gossip are the third type of unskillful speech. Words of this nature cause disharmony and the loss of friends. It's interesting to consider why gossip is so prevalent. Why do we enjoy it so much? In some way, does it reaffirm and strengthen our sense of self?

Some years ago I was being interviewed for a book, and the interviewer kept asking leading questions about people I knew, waiting for me to air my various views and opinions. Fortunately, I could see what was happening, and despite a certain seductive temptation I refrained from indulging this type of wrong speech. When I later saw everything I had said in print, I realized I saved myself much regret. It's possible to make choices about what we say; words need not simply tumble out of our mouths.

Our speech can also be a kind of gossip about ourselves. Sometimes our talk is overly self-referential, always turning conversations back to ourselves. Do we find ways for taking center stage in our communications, for taking center stage in our lives? It would be insightful to look at our motivations at these times. The poet Antonio Machado suggested an antidote to this habit of speech: "If you want to talk, first ask a question, then listen."

The last in this list of unskillful speech actions is *frivolous and useless talk*. How often do we say things that really are of no use at all? Sometimes, in various social interactions, I make the effort to be mindful of my intention to speak, trying to be aware before the words come out. In these situations I notice that there is often an impulse to add something quite needless to the conversation. This kind of talk is enervating; what a relief it is to simply let these thoughts go. If the pattern of frivolous talk is strong, slowly our words become worthless, losing our own respect as well as that of others.

Sometimes quite bad consequences come from impulsive, frivolous words. The following is an incident that happened a year before September 11th. In today's climate, the consequences of such frivolous speech would be considerably greater. After many weeks of planning, a friend of mine was leaving on a trip to Bali, Indonesia. He was at Kennedy airport in New York, just settling into an upgraded first-class seat on the plane. Having previously injured his hand, he had some kind of plastic balls for exercising it. When the flight attendant came by to offer some drinks and newspapers, she asked him about the balls. Without thinking, my friend replied in jest, "Oh, it's plastique," which, as most of us know, is a favorite explosive of terrorists. Within minutes, security guards and FBI agents were on the plane escorting my friend to a holding cell; the airline personnel vowed he would never fly out of JFK again. Hours later he finally convinced them that, although he had spoken stupidly, he had no evil intent. It took him days to get back in the good graces of the airline and to rebook a flight.

Sometimes words just slip out. And when we're not mindful, it happens again and again. As this same friend was returning home, sitting in the airport in Bali, he struck up a conversation with another traveler. Intending to tell the story of his New York adventure, he blurted out to his new acquaintance, "Do you know you're talking with a terrorist?" Fortunately, he immediately explained himself. But if there had been security people nearby, who knows where he would be now?

When we take a few moments to investigate the feelings behind our words, we can uncover motives that are often hidden or confused. Self-righteous words sometimes mask anger; angry words can cover self-righteousness. Sometimes we engage in useless banter out of a feeling of unworthiness or a need for approval and attention. It's not without cause that the Buddha included right speech as one of the steps in the Eightfold Path to awakening. It is an amazingly fruitful arena of exploration, and a place where mindfulness can be practiced throughout the day.

Actions of the Mind

The last three unskillful actions the Buddha pointed out are actions of mind. These are subtler than actions of body or speech and take keen investigation to explore and understand. The first of them is *covetousness*, the wanting mind, the feeling that we never have enough. In the framework of the Buddhist cosmology and the different realms of existence, the extreme of this covetous mind state typifies the hungry-ghost realm. Hungry ghosts are often depicted as having huge stomachs and pinhole mouths, indicating that they are incapable of ever feeling satisfied. In our own culture, we might call it "catalogue consciousness," obsessively rifling through the pages to see what else we might want. It's "wanting to want," and it's a disease our culture keeps nourishing.

Covetousness keeps the mind agitated and unhappy, far from the peace of contentment. It's interesting to note that in another venerable list of actions to avoid, the Ten Commandments, covetousness appears twice. We shouldn't underestimate this habit of mind, which, unnoticed, can easily lead to the suffering of envy, jealousy, and endless dissatisfaction. Different wisdom traditions simply remind us that we have the power to refrain from actions that cause suffering. We can be happy; it is up to us.

The next of the unwholesome actions of mind is *ill will*, with its many attendant variations: anger, hatred, impatience, and sorrow—all forms of aversion. We can notice the feelings of contraction and hardening of the heart when we get lost in or identified with mind states of ill will. These states of aversion arise when we don't get what we want, or when we do get what we don't want. They may come in response to present unpleasantness, such as pain, certain distressing emotions, or difficult life situations. Ill will of one kind or another can also arise when we remember certain past events or anticipate future ones. Sometimes just imagining something happening makes us angry or upset. Mark Twain noted this phenomenon with his usual clear wit: "Some of the worst things in my life never happened."

Questions often come up about grief and sorrow. We don't often associate aversion with these states, yet the Buddha included them in this category. We need great delicacy here, so there is a willingness to investigate the roots of these emotions and, at the

same time, to have the space to accept and feel them fully. S
and grief arise from loss of some kind. What is our relationship to
the experience of loss, which is really another word for change? Is
there aversion to it? Is there attachment to what was lost, whether
it is a person, possession, or situation in our lives?

I was first struck by the difference between loss and sorrow
when I happened to reflect on and connect two different teachings in the Buddhist texts. One is a story revealing the Buddha's
own keen awareness of the feeling of loss. At the death of his
chief disciples, Sariputta and Moggallana, the Buddha remarked
that it was as if the light of the sun and the moon had gone out
from the sky, so great was their contribution to the teachings.
This is a very poignant reflection on the magnitude of the loss.

The second teaching comes from the *Satipatthana Sutta*, the
discourse on the foundations of mindfulness. In this sutta, the
Buddha declares the fruits of the practice: "This is the way for
the purification of beings, for the overcoming of sorrow and
lamentation, for the disappearance of pain and grief, for reaching the Noble Path, for the realization of Nibbana—namely, the
four foundations of mindfulness."

So how could the Buddha have felt the loss of his great and
close disciples, yet at the same time declare that awakening leads
to the overcoming of sorrow and the disappearance of grief?
Can we experience loss without the attendant sorrow or grief?
Perhaps it is acceptance and mindfulness of the feeling of loss
that make this possible, and it is nonacceptance that rebounds
into grief. It would be interesting to explore not simply the
acceptance of the loss itself, which is often a process over time,
but an acceptance of the feeling of loss, which can happen in
any moment. When we investigate our relationship to different
emotions, our practice opens us to new levels of understanding.
What may seem impossible, or even unnatural, at one level may
become the norm at another.

At the same time, we need to be right where we are, not living in an idealized pretense of where we'd like to be. Most of us

have probably not yet overcome attachment and aversion, pride and fear, sorrow and grief. The question then remains, can we just be with these feelings skillfully? Can we be open without indulging and experience them without holding on? It is finding the balance between working with these emotions as an ongoing process of acceptance and letting go and exploring the possibility of cutting through our attachments in just a moment of clear understanding.

Verses in the *Sutta Nipata*, one of the oldest collections in the entire Buddhist canon and considered by many to be the closest to the Buddha's actual words, give clear advice about letting go of some of these emotions. Here is a translation adapted from H. Saddhatissa:

> When a house is burning, the fire is extinguished by water. In the same way, the wise person, learned, skilful and self-reliant, will extinguish sorrow as soon as it arises, like the wind blowing away a ball of cotton.
>
> The person who seeks his own happiness should remove the self-placed dart of grieving, desiring and despair.
>
> The person who has removed the dart, who is free of clinging and grief, having obtained peace of mind, is still.

The last of the ten unwholesome actions is *wrong view*, basic misperceptions that become the cause of difficulty and suffering in our lives. One wrong view is the belief that there is no karmic result from either good or bad actions, and therefore it doesn't matter what we do. When we have this view we are trying to navigate through life without the light of understanding of what brings happiness and what brings suffering. We then take many missteps and go in wrong directions. When this wrong view is present in the mind, we don't stop to consider the results of actions, where they lead, and whether that is where we really want to go.

Another aspect of wrong view is the belief that there are no enlightened beings, those who have realized for themselves the end of suffering. For many years I read this teaching and passed over it quickly. It just did not seem as important as other kinds of basic misperceptions. But the view that there are no liberated beings in the world has greater implications than we may think, because, by extension, it disallows the possibility of freedom for us. It often becomes personalized as feelings of unworthiness, feelings that might have been conditioned by particular circumstances in our lives, but that don't reflect our deepest, truest nature.

Someone once said to the Dalai Lama, "I do not feel worthwhile as a person. How can I work on this as a beginning meditation student?"

The Dalai Lama replied, "You should not be discouraged. Your feeling, 'I am of no value' is wrong. Absolutely wrong. You are deceiving yourself."

Seeing unworthiness as a wrong view of ourselves helps make it something we can work with. Instead of thinking there is something fundamentally wrong with the way we are, we see it is the very thought of being unworthy that is the problem. When we honor the genuine wisdom in others, we begin to honor the same possibility for wisdom in ourselves. This honoring of wisdom is a powerful antidote to feelings of unworthiness, discouragement, and despair; it is the great gift of the Dharma to us all.

Another aspect of wrong view that we will discuss in much greater detail in later chapters is the deeply conditioned sense of "I," of self. On the relative level, of course, we move and speak and act as individuals, as selves. Yet on a deeper level, and with close attention, we can see through this appearance and experience the place of nonseparation from others and from the world. This is the realization of selflessness.

THE TEN UNWHOLESOME ACTIONS, THEN, ARE THREE OF body: killing, stealing, sexual misconduct; four of speech: lying, harsh words, gossip, and useless talk; and three of mind:

covetousness, ill will, and wrong view. The Buddha highlighted these for us out of his compassion and care. They are dangers. They do harm, causing suffering to others and having a deleterious effect on our own happiness. Reading the Buddha's admonitions to refrain from these actions is like coming across a sign on the beach saying, "Danger. Strong Undertow." We were walking along the beautiful beach about to dive into the inviting ocean when we encountered the life-saving warning. This is the Buddha as lifeguard, putting up the notices.

In this very straightforward teaching, the Buddha helps us understand the practice of freedom with a mature and long-ranging vision. Freedom is not simply doing what we want when we want it. That is addiction. Freedom is the wisdom to choose wisely. If we wish to be free of the causes of suffering, these ten are the unwholesome actions to avoid.

So we train ourselves in this first aspect of the timeless Dharma—avoiding what is unskillful. With his characteristic modesty and good humor, the Dalai Lama spoke of his own training. He said he came from a part of Tibet where people are naturally short-tempered, but that over the years he had trained himself to let go when this state arose. Sometimes anger or disturbance would come for just a few moments, but then his mind would become calm again. He said that even though he has been a lazy practitioner because of lack of time (getting up at four each morning to meditate for a few hours before beginning the day!), still he has seen much improvement.

No one can practice for us. The Buddhas just point the way.

SIX

ACTING FOR THE GOOD

Do not take lightly small good deeds,
Believing they can hardly help.
For drops of water one by one
In time can fill a giant pot.

—PATRUL RINPOCHE,
THE WORDS OF MY PERFECT TEACHER

WE MOVE FROM THE FIRST OF THE TEACHINGS OF ALL THE
Buddhas, doing no harm, to the second: acting for the good.
This principle of One Dharma, common to all traditions, highlights the positive actions we undertake both for our own welfare
and for the benefit and well-being of others. Actions for the
good accumulate what is called "merit"—one of the most commonly misunderstood concepts in Buddhism.

"Merit" is the usual translation of the Pali word *punna*,
which more literally means "virtue" or that which purifies and
cleanses the life stream, bringing good results. Meritorious
actions hold the key to happiness in our lives. They are the
seeds of happiness of all kinds, both temporary worldly success
and all spiritual accomplishments. It is accumulated merit that

makes them possible. But we mistake the meaning of merit when we use this idea to strengthen some sense of self, of someone behind all the actions acquiring gold stars for good behavior. Rather, the notion of merit comes from a profound understanding of interdependence, the understanding that everything arises from causes. Meritorious actions are simply those that have the power to bring happiness and blessings in our lives.

On the night of his enlightenment, when the Bodhisattva saw with his refined vision beings taking birth and dying, over and over again, driven by the winds of their karma, he understood clearly that different kinds of actions bring their respective results. From this perspective, we then investigate what actions and motivations are the causes and conditions for genuine happiness. We need to explore our own minds and lives to see for ourselves.

Robert Thurman, a Tibetan practitioner and scholar, gives a good example of how our own happiness is inextricably intertwined with everyone else's. He asked that we imagine being on a subway car full of people—for all the rest of time! Some people on the car are quite content sitting there, reading their newspapers or eating their lunch. Others are agitated, upset, or angry for one reason or another, creating a lot of tension in the car. Given that these are our companions for eternity, rather than just until the next stop, what is the wisest course of action? What will bring the greatest happiness? Obviously, if in some way we can alleviate the distress of our fellow passengers, everyone enjoys the greater peace and harmony that ensue. Our own happiness ultimately depends on the happiness of others. We just often forget that we're all on this journey together.

As he does with so much of what we encounter on the spiritual path, the Buddha offers guidelines for this very important investigation of "acting for the good." One way of understanding it is as the renunciation, or nondoing, of the ten unwholesome activities discussed in the last chapter. Another way expresses it in positive terms, such as reverence for life, generosity, lovingkindness, and so forth. Still another frame of reference talks of cultivating six particular skillful actions, beginning with how we live in the world and culminating in meditative wisdom.

SIX SKILLFUL ACTIONS

Generosity heads almost every list of actions for the good. For many people it is the easiest one to appreciate and develop because it brings such immediate delight to our lives. Generosity enacts the quality of nongreed; it is a willingness to give, to share, to let go. It may be the giving of time, energy, resources, love, and even, in rare cases, one's own life for the benefit and welfare of others. Generosity weakens the tendency of attachment and grasping and is intimately connected with the feeling of lovingkindness. In a wonderful kind of reciprocity, we are inspired to give because of loving feeling, and in the act of giving we feel more love. Generosity becomes stronger and more delightful the more we engage in it. As a training exercise for us in generosity, we might practice acting on our impulses to give, rather than letting them pass by.

The Path of Purification, an ancient commentary on the earliest Buddhist teachings, describes the person with a highly developed practice of generosity as being someone who not only gives when opportunities present themselves, but also delights in being asked for whatever is needed. Such a person finds joy in each opportunity to give.

As mentioned previously, there have been many Buddhas, Awakened Ones, in the past and there will be many more to come in the future. A story of a previous Buddha named Kassapa and a poor potter illustrates the delight in generosity. The story comes from a direct translation of the Pali texts, and so it gives us some feeling for the rhythm and language of the original oral teachings.

The king of Kasi (Benares) had three times invited the Buddha Kassapa to accept a residence for the Rains Retreat.

Each time the Blessed One refused, saying that his residence for the Rains had already been provided for. The king then asked whether the Buddha had a better supporter than himself.

"I do, great king," the Buddha Kassapa replied. "There is a market town . . . where a potter named Ghatikara lives. He is my supporter, my chief supporter. . . . The potter Ghatikara has gone for refuge to the Buddha, the Dhamma, and the Sangha. He abstains from killing living beings, from taking what is not given, from misconduct in sensual pleasures, from false speech, and from wine, liquor, and intoxicants, which are the basis of negligence. He has perfect confidence in the Buddha, the Dhamma, and the Sangha, and he possesses the virtues loved by noble ones. . . . He eats only in one part of the day, he observes celibacy, he is virtuous, of good character. He has laid aside gems and gold, he has given up gold and silver . . . and when he has made a pot he says: 'Let anyone who likes set down some selected rice or selected beans or selected lentils, and let him take away whatever he likes.' He supports his blind and aged parents. . . .

"On one occasion when I was living nearby, it being morning, I dressed, and taking my bowl and outer robe, I went to the potter Ghatikara's parents and asked them: 'Where has the potter gone, please?'

"'Venerable sir, your supporter has gone out; but take rice from the cauldron and sauce from the saucepan and eat.'

"I did so and went away. Then the potter Ghatikara went to his parents and asked: 'Who has taken rice from the cauldron and sauce from the saucepan, eaten, and gone away?'

"'My dear, the Blessed One Kassapa, accomplished and fully enlightened, did.'

"Then the potter Ghatikara thought: 'It is a gain for me, it is a great gain for me that the Blessed One Kassapa, accomplished and fully enlightened, relies on me thus.' And rapture and happiness never left him for half a month or his parents for a week. . . .

"On another occasion when I was living at Vebhalinga my hut leaked. Then I addressed the bhikkhus thus: 'Go, bhikkhus, and find out if there is any grass at the potter Ghatikara's house.'

"'Venerable sir, there is no grass at the potter Ghatikara's house; there is the grass thatch on his roof.'

"'Go, bhikkhus, and remove the grass from the potter Ghatikara's house.'

"They did so. Then the potter Ghatikara's parents asked the bhikkhus: 'Who is removing the grass from the house?'

"'Sister, the hut of the Blessed One Kassapa, accomplished and fully enlightened, is leaking.'

"'Take it, venerable sirs, take it and bless you!'

"Then the potter Ghatikara went to his parents and asked: 'Who has removed the grass from the roof?'

"'The bhikkhus did, my dear; the hut of the Blessed One Kassapa, accomplished and fully enlightened, is leaking.'

"Then the potter Ghatikara thought: 'It is a gain for me, it is a great gain for me that the Blessed One Kassapa, accomplished and fully enlightened, relies on me thus!' And the rapture and happiness never left him for half a month or his parents for a week. Then that house remained three whole months with the sky for a roof, and yet no rain came in. Such is the potter Ghatikara."

The story then goes on to describe in detail some of the more immediate and abundant fruits of Ghatikara's offering. The king of Kasi himself could not match the profound faith and loving generosity of this simple (and, as it turns out, quite enlightened) potter.

The second skillful action is *morality* (*sila* in Pali). In his praise of Ghatikara above, the Buddha Kassapa reiterates the five basic precepts of nonharming: refraining from killing, stealing, sexual misconduct, lying, and taking intoxicants. Sometimes the practice of *sila*, abiding by the five precepts, is easy—we're simply doing what seems natural to us. At other times, though, the choices before us may be difficult and following a basic precept may mean the renunciation of some desire, a conscious act of restraint. At these times, *sila* becomes a true practice of transformation. Here's where we have the chance to strengthen our proverbial moral fiber.

Understanding *sila* as a practice rests on realizing that the happiness or unhappiness of the moment should not be the sole deciding factor for making our choices. Sometimes pleasant experience in the moment leads to unwanted results in the future—witness the effects of different kinds of addictions or unwanted pregnancies. And sometimes unpleasant or painful experiences in the present lead to good results later on. Think of the struggle of an athlete training for the Olympics or someone on his or her first meditation retreat. The guide for our actions should not simply be whether something is pleasant or unpleasant right now, but whether wholesome qualities of mind and heart are being strengthened. It is those qualities that are the source of our more lasting happiness.

As we practice *sila*, it becomes a strong and purifying force in our lives, benefiting both others and ourselves in so many ways. The Buddha talked of morality as being the true beauty of a person. Unfortunately, we often place importance on outer beauty and often overlook the goodness that really shines on the inside of a person. *Sila* also gives strength to our aspirations. It is the karmic force that brings us desired results.

When *sila* is strong, we are saying with our actions that no one need fear us. This is one of the greatest contributions we can give to the world, for our nonharming offers the gift of safety and trust to all those around us. And last, morality brings us the peace of nonremorse. Through our commitment and practice of nonharming—in actions of body, speech, and mind—the suffering of regret, which can be such a powerfully negative force in our lives, does not agitate our minds. When our minds are not agitated, concentration comes more easily. From concentration comes the birth of wisdom.

Although we all have been responsible for many unskillful actions in the past, the great power and beauty of moral behavior is that we draw strength and ease from it as soon as we recommit ourselves to this life of nonharming. Perhaps the Dalai Lama best summed up the importance of *sila* when he said, "My true religion is kindness." One aim of this wholesome action is to make this religion our own as well.

The next two wholesome actions are *respect* and *service*. Often we respect outer things—money, power, fame, beauty—or the people who have them. But it's possible to see past these enticements to what is of greater and more enduring value. As we practice the four mind-changing reflections—on our precious human birth, impermanence, the law of karma, and the defects of samsara—they generate a great respect for the Dharma and for the efforts we make to purify our own hearts and minds. Respect leads to caring—a quality of impeccability in what we do. How often do we rush through the day, not paying attention to even the simplest things? When we slow down, even a little, we connect with a deeper level of experience. Georgia O'Keefe expressed this very well: "Still in a way, nobody sees a flower really. It is so small. We haven't time and to see takes time—like to have a friend takes time."

Respect for the Dharma and our practice also leads to greater care in our relationships. We become more aware of and sensitive to the people around us. One of the joys of reading the words of the Buddha is that they point us, often in obvious ways that we overlook or forget, in the direction of happiness.

One story tells of monks who were living together in a wooded park. One day, the Buddha came to visit and said he hoped that they were keeping well, that they were comfortable and were receiving sufficient food. He then went on to say, "I hope, Anuruddha [one of the monks], that you are all living in concord, with mutual appreciation, without disputing, blending like milk and water, viewing each other with kindly eyes."

Anuruddha replied, "Surely, venerable sir, we are living in concord, with mutual appreciation, without disputing, blending like milk and water, viewing each other with kindly eyes."

The Buddha then asked the key question: "But, Anuruddha, how do you live thus?" Here we get to the crux of our own living in concord and harmony through a profoundly simple message that comes down to us through twenty-five hundred years of human society. Anuruddha answered:

> Venerable sir, as to that, I think thus: "It is a gain for me, it is a great gain for me, that I am living with such companions in the holy life." I maintain bodily acts of lovingkindness toward these venerable ones, both openly and privately; I maintain verbal acts of lovingkindness toward them both openly and privately; I maintain mental acts of lovingkindness toward them both openly and privately. I consider: "Why should I not set aside what I wish to do and do what these venerable ones wish to do?" Then I set aside what I wish to do and do what these venerable ones wish to do. We are different in body, venerable sir, but one in mind.

The Buddha, and many others, spoke of respecting the wise and, what might sometimes be a cultural stretch for us, respecting one's parents and other elders. The Buddha commented that we could carry our parents on our shoulders for the rest of their lives and still not repay the gift of our precious human birth. Although our culture doesn't value parental respect to the degree that Eastern cultures do, cultivating gratitude opens many doors in the relationship. There are often complicating circumstances that can't be ignored, but deepening our relationship to elders has far-reaching implications. By giving respect to that which is worthy of it, we align ourselves with those values. Respect and faith nourish each other and give birth to many skillful actions.

As we foster the quality of respect in our lives, we also begin to see the world in a different light. The tone of caring that arises from giving respect can transform how we interact with society. Before our eyes we see the ways in which we can offer our care. We begin to explore the possibilities of service, of taking an active role in seeing what needs doing and lending our energy to those endeavors. Although sometimes people create a divide between spiritual practice and social engagement, we are seeing more and more clearly that they are unified in the flowering of wisdom and compassion. Compassion motivates us to act, and wisdom ensures the means are effective.

The Dalai Lama wrote:

> I, too, am firmly of the opinion that those who sincerely practice Buddha Dharma must also serve society. Too often we make what we call "the happiness of all sentient beings" the object of our prayers and meditations, yet when we rise from our meditation cushions we fail to give practical help to our neighbors and others in need. If we are to fulfill our altruistic wish, we cannot discriminate between spirituality and our life in society. Without the support of our fellow beings we could not practice at all, and without a concern for their welfare, our practice has little meaning.

Careful attention is needed so that we do not foster the division of meditation and social action by making judgments about what other people should be doing with their lives. We each have our own rhythm of inner work and outer service. This rhythm may be one of weeks, months, years, or even lifetimes. When we read of the many past lives of the Buddha, when he was off practicing in some remote mountain cave, in the context of that one life it may seem like self-centered spiritual striving: "What's that old hermit doing for anyone else?" But in the context of that solitary practice being part of his path to Buddhahood—and all the immense compassionate activity that flowed from his awakening—then we understand the deep motivation of compassion that fueled those many lifetimes of effort.

When we take just a snapshot picture of a person's experience or path, as our judging mind likes to do, we may get a very distorted view of the larger picture. Respect for all wholesome actions holds the key to wide tolerance and openhearted appreciation.

Hearing the Dharma and sharing it with others is the fifth skillful action. Words have power, and many people have become enlightened simply by attentive listening to the teachings. Listening itself is an art. Often as we listen we are busy with our own thoughts, judgments, and reactions. But when we listen with a still and concentrated mind, it's possible to actually be responsive to what the words are saying. Sometimes deep insights come in a flash, unexpectedly.

I had a powerful personal experience of this truth. A few weeks before the end of my Peace Corps time in Thailand, I was sitting quietly in a friend's garden listening to him read from a Tibetan text called, in that early translation, *The Tibetan Book of the Great Liberation.* My mind had become quite concentrated and at one point, when the text was speaking of the "unborn nature of the mind," there was a sudden and spontaneous experience of the mind opening . . . to zero. This momentary opening to the "unmanifest," a reality beyond the ordinary mind and body, had the force of a lightning bolt shattering the solidified illusion of self. Immediately following this, a phrase kept repeating in my mind, "There's no me, there's no me." This experience radically changed my understanding of things. Of course, since then, feelings or thoughts of "me," of a sense of self, have arisen many times, but, still, the deep knowing remains that even the *sense of self* is selfless—that it's just another thought.

Just as listening to the Dharma can provoke immediate understandings as well as provide seeds for insights to come, so too do speaking and sharing the Dharma actively purify the mind. I've noticed many times being extremely tired before giving a dharma talk and feeling completely energized afterward. It is as if the wisdom of the Dharma illumines both the listener and the speaker. One Sutta describes it this way: "Monks, there are these four radiances. What four? The radiance of the moon, of the sun, of fire, and of wisdom. Of these four, Monks, the radiance of wisdom is the chief." The Buddha remarked that the gift of Dharma is the highest gift, for giver and receiver both.

The last of these wholesome actions is *meditation*, the development of tranquillity and insight. Meditation begins with calming the mind and collecting the attention. The importance of this is revealed at the very beginning of our practice—it is often the first insight we gain when we begin to practice meditation. We see for ourselves how difficult the mind is to control. The mind is so slippery. We feel a breath or two, and then the mind wanders. We become seduced or distracted by thoughts, plans, and memories—sometimes not even pleasant ones. We often relive old arguments or hurts. We hop on a train of association not knowing that we've hopped on and having no idea where the train is going. Somewhere down the line we wake up from the dream of our thoughts, often in a completely different mental environment. Perhaps we have become entangled in some drama, some strong emotion, contracted in a strong sense of self, of ego. And all the time it is just the play of our minds.

Training the mind is a bit like training a young puppy to sit. You sit it down and a moment later it's jumping all over you, licking your face and hands. You sit it down again, "Sit, sit," and again in just a few moments it's up and running about. But with some gentle persistence and dedication, over time, the puppy does learn to stay and sit. Our minds are very much like this little puppy.

Verses from the *Dhammapada* remind us that this wandering mind was the same in the time of the Buddha as it is for us today:

*The mind is restless, unsteady, hard to
guard, hard to control. The wise one
makes it straight, like a fletcher
straightens an arrow.*

* * *

How good it is to rein the mind,
Which is unruly, capricious, rushing wherever it pleases.
The mind so harnessed will bring one happiness.

Your worst enemy cannot harm you
As much as your own unguarded thoughts.
A well-directed mind creates more happiness
Than even the loving actions of your parents.

So we begin with a very simple object of attention, like the breath, and train ourselves to return to it even as we get distracted over and over again. This first insight into the habit of distraction leads us to understand the value and importance of steadying our attention, because the worlds we create in ourselves and around us all have their origins in our own minds. How many different mind-worlds do we inhabit in our thoughts, even between one breath and the next? And how many actions do we take because of these unnoticed thoughts?

By first taking a particular object of concentration and then training the mind to stay focused on it, we can develop calmness and tranquillity. The object may be the breath, a sound or mantra, a visual image, or certain reflections, all of which serve to concentrate the mind. At first, this requires the effort of continually returning each time the mind wanders off. With practice, though, the mind becomes trained, and then rests quite easily in the chosen object.

In addition to the feelings of restfulness and peace, the state of concentration also becomes the basis for deepening insight and wisdom. We find ourselves opening to the world's suffering as well as to its great beauty. Through the power of increased awareness, simple experience often becomes magically alive: the silhouette of a branch against the night sky or trees swaying in the invisible wind. The way that we sense the world becomes purified, our perception of the world transformed. Marcel Proust wrote, "The real voyage of discovery consists not in seeing new landscapes but in having new eyes."

Generosity, morality, respect, service, listening to the Dharma, and meditation—these are actions for the good. Each one is a practice that can be cultivated and further refined, becoming the causes for our own happiness and the happiness of others. These acts for the good become our gift to the world.

SEVEN

PURIFYING THE MIND

Which is worth more, a crowd of thousands,
or your own genuine solitude?
Freedom, or power over an entire nation.

A little while alone in your room
will prove more valuable than anything else
that could ever be given you.

—RUMI, *THE ESSENTIAL RUMI*

THE LAST PART OF THE BUDDHA'S TEACHINGS EXPRESSED
in the *Dhammapada* verse—avoid what is unskillful, do what is
good, purify the mind—points to a vast array of skillful means
that purify the mind of qualities that cloud our vision and pre-
vent clear seeing. Within the Theravada tradition there are forty
traditional subjects of concentration and more than fifty different ways of practicing insight. In other schools of Buddhism
there are even more. How do we find our way through this abundance of possibilities? Trungpa Rinpoche, a brilliant and creative
Tibetan master, in reply to a question about finding one's teacher
and path, said, "It's best, perhaps, to follow the pretense of acci-

dent." We read, explore, stumble upon, try out, are led to, and somehow connect—in ways different for each one of us—with a particular teacher or practice that inspires us.

There is a certain mystery to the process of finding one's path, although when we look back at our own spiritual journey, it often seems as if there were an underlying order all along. We need to simply trust the integrity of our seeking. Everything follows from that. We'll know when the connection is there.

When I first went to India in 1967 to look for a teacher, I had been given the names of various people, from Tibetan lamas to Hindu gurus, and many places to go to. After finding myself with a summer sleeping bag in a Himalayan winter (all the lamas having gone south) and carrying bricks on my head in an ashram on the Indian plains, I decided to return to Thailand, where I had been during my time in the Peace Corps. Maybe I would find something there. But just at this point, something quite strange happened. I was in New Delhi, walking down Janpath Lane to the airline office, when some force or energy stopped me in my tracks. I was simply unable to take another step forward. Rather than just stand there, I returned to my hotel wondering about this rather peculiar event. The next day, I decided to go to Benares instead. After a few days of wandering in this Hindu holy city, I resolved to go back to New Delhi and try again. But in a rickshaw going to the train station, the thought of Bodh Gaya unexpectedly popped into my mind. Maybe I would go there, to the place of the Buddha's enlightenment, and sit myself under the great Bodhi Tree. At the last moment, I changed my plans and traveled the five hours to this unique place.

The train stopped in Gaya, an ancient city in Northern India, where Hindu pilgrims come each year for a festival honoring one's parents and ancestors. I made my way through the crowd of porters and other travelers to the bicycle rickshaws waiting outside the station and began a journey that would transform my life. After winding through the narrow lanes of the city, the way opened to a pastoral beauty that had probably not changed much in centuries. The road to Bodh Gaya skirted villages, fields, and clusters of huge mango trees along a dry riverbed. People, water buffalo, and vehicles of all kinds and vintages did a roadway dance, somehow managing to avoid collision. As we approached the village, I could just make out the top of the majestic Mahabodhi temple, which stands at the site of the Buddha's awakening. This was a place that would become a refuge of wakefulness and inspiration for me during the next seven years.

I settled at the Burmese vihara, a rest house at the edge of the village, which had originally been built for Burmese pilgrims. In those years, Burma was closed to most travel, both in and out of the country, so the Burmese vihara became the place of choice for Western dharma seekers. At that time, there were only a few Europeans in residence, and they quickly offered to take me to their teacher, Anagarika Munindra. He had recently returned from nine years of practice and study in Burma to begin teaching in the land of the Buddha's birth.

One day, as we were sitting in a small group on the open roof of the vihara, Munindraji ("-ji" is a suffix of respect in Hindi) asked each one of us, "Why do you want to practice?"

For me the aspiration was clear: "For liberation."

He then went on to say something that sealed my decision to stay and practice for as long as I could. "If you want to understand your mind, sit down and observe it." It was this clear, commonsense, undogmatic approach that so inspired me. There was nothing to join, no rituals to observe, no beliefs to follow. The mysteries of the mind would reveal themselves simply through the power of my own growing awareness.

The Practice of Mindfulness

Mindfulness holds a central place of importance in every Buddhist path. Indeed, it is what makes any spiritual practice possible. Mindfulness is the quality of mind that notices what is present, without judgment, without interference. It is like a mirror that clearly reflects what comes before it. Munindraji summed up this quality with one simple expression: knowing things as they are.

Mindfulness serves many functions and is therefore likened to an executive's chief of staff (actually, the Pali texts liken it to a king's minister-of-all-work). If you want something done, that's the person you need to go to. Mindfulness helps distinguish the good from the bad, the worthy from the unworthy. It keeps different wholesome states of mind in balance, working together in harmony. It also contributes to wise recollection. Without mindfulness, we don't know what our minds are doing and so are often lost in confusion. The following verses, from a spontaneous dharma song by Nyoshul Khen Rinpoche, proclaim the great virtues of this quality:

> Mindfulness is the root of Dharma.
> Mindfulness is the body of practice.
> Mindfulness is the fortress of the mind.
> Mindfulness is the aid to the wisdom of innate wakefulness.

> Lack of mindfulness will allow the negative forces to overcome you.
> Without mindfulness you will be swept away by laziness.
> Lack of mindfulness is the creator of evil deeds.
> Without mindfulness and presence of mind, nothing can be accomplished.
> Lack of mindfulness piles up lots of shit.
> Without mindfulness you sleep in an ocean of piss.

> Without mindfulness you are a heartless zombie, a walking corpse.
> Dear Dharma friends, please be mindful!

By the aspiration of the holy lamas, Buddhas, bodhisattvas, and
  lineage masters,
May all vajra [vajrayana; dharma] friends attain stable
  mindfulness and ascend the throne
Of perfect Awakening.

Different traditions talk of mindfulness in different ways: sometimes as a quality to be cultivated, sometimes as an aspect of the innate wakefulness of mind, often as both. Dzogchen, the Tibetan teaching of the "Natural Great Perfection," calls these two aspects fabricated and unfabricated mindfulness. Fabricated mindfulness is the conditioned state of mind that makes an effort to stay attentive. Although there is some sense of duality here—someone doing something—we need this kind of mindfulness to bring us back to the moment. On a more subtle level of fabrication, mindfulness is steady, but there is still some sense of a reference point, of an observer. Unfabricated mindfulness is a quality of the Nature of Mind, what Dzogchen calls the original wakefulness of the Natural State. It is called "unfabricated" because, according to Dzogchen teachings, this kind of mindfulness is not something we have created; rather, it is like the capacity of a mirror to reflect what comes before it. That capacity is in the very nature of the mirror itself.

These two types of mindfulness work in harmony. It is the rare person who can simply abide uninterruptedly in unfabricated mindfulness, without the support of appropriate effort. Unfabricated mindfulness itself is effortless, but without training our recognition of it is short-lived. In one way or another, we need to make mindfulness—the quality of being present in the moment, awake to what is happening—the heart of our practice. Tulku Urgyen Rinpoche, a great Dzogchen master of the last century, taught, "There is one thing we always need, and that is the watchman named mindfulness, the guard who is on the lookout for when we get carried away in mindlessness."

FOUR FOUNDATIONS OF MINDFULNESS

The Buddha first gave the "Discourse on the Four Foundations of Mindfulness," the *Satipatthana Sutta*, in the land of the Kurus, a prosperous region in Northern India. The people there were particularly blessed with good health, comfortable conditions, and a love of wisdom that made their minds receptive to this direct teaching on the way to liberation. It is said in the Pali commentaries that the village people there would ask each other, "Which foundation of mindfulness do you practice?" as they gathered by the wells or meeting places. It was to such people that the Buddha taught this precious Sutta.

It is mindfulness that holds the promise of freedom. At the end of the *Satipatthana Sutta*, the Buddha declares:

> Bhikkhus, if anyone should develop these four foundations of mindfulness in such a way for seven years, one of two fruits could be expected for him: either final knowledge here and now, or if there is a trace of clinging left, nonreturn [the penultimate stage of enlightenment].

The Buddha goes on to qualify the length of time, saying that if anyone should develop these foundations of mindfulness for six years, or five years, or any amount of time all the way down to seven days, one of two fruits could be expected—full enlightenment here and now or, if some trace of clinging remains, the next to last stage of awakening.

What, then, are the four foundations of mindfulness? The Sutta describes four comprehensive fields of attention, and then further delineates each of them in some detail. They are mindfulness of the body, mindfulness of feelings, mindfulness of the mind and mental states, and mindfulness of the Dharma. This last category includes some lists of the basic teachings, such as the five hindrances, the seven qualities of enlightenment, the Four Noble Truths, the six sense bases, and so forth.

There are many methods for putting this teaching into practice. Some methods emphasize one of the four fields of mindfulness as the gateway to the others. Some include all four foundations right from the beginning. Altogether, there are more than fifty different practices outlined in this Sutta. The meditations that derive from these foundations of mindfulness are called *vipassana* (Pali for "insight," or more literally, "seeing clearly"), and in one form or another—and by whatever name—are found in all the major Buddhist traditions. It is the basic practice of paying attention, of resting in awareness, of listening, which is central to any path of awakening.

How to Practice

How do we begin? The meditation practice presented here comes primarily from the Burmese tradition of Mahasi Sayadaw, although it is flavored by some teachings from other schools. We start with sitting meditation, which can serve as the foundation for mindfulness in all other postures and activities as well. Find a comfortable posture, either sitting cross-legged on a cushion, kneeling on a meditation bench, or sitting in a chair. Keep your back straight, but without strain or tension. Let your hands rest easily on your knees or lap. It may take some time and experimentation to find the posture that is most suitable for you, but as you practice you soon "find your seat." Gently close your eyes and let your attention settle into the awareness of your body posture. Stay relaxed, simply feeling your body just as it is. You can make a very soft, silent mental note, or label, "Sitting," to help keep your mind connected with this experience.

As you relax more and more into the awareness of your body, begin to open to the experience of hearing. Notice whatever sounds appear. They may be loud and, at first, disruptive ones. They may be soft background noises. It may be the sound of silence. Simply listen, as if you were hearing your favorite music. Don't think about what is making the sound or anticipate what might be coming. There is just the vibration of sound, appearing and disappearing, in the open clear space of your awareness. You may begin to notice certain things about this experience. The sounds seem to arise quite spontaneously and, when the mind is undistracted, be heard quite effortlessly. The nature of the mind is awareness. When we're not lost in thought or daydreams, we hear all the sounds with quite amazing clarity and ease.

Stay grounded in the awareness of your body posture, opening to sounds as they come and go. From this place of open, spacious awareness begin to connect with the feeling of each breath as it enters and leaves the body. Let each breath come in its own time, in its own manner. There is no "right" breath. This is not a breathing exercise; it is an exercise in awareness. Notice how the sensations of the breath appear in just the same way sounds do, spontaneously arising, effortlessly known. Where in the body do you feel the breath most clearly? Is it at the nostrils as the air flows past, or is it in the movement of the chest or the abdomen? Practice keeping the attention steady at the place where the sensations of the breath are generally most predominant. Later on, it's possible to simply be with each breath wherever it appears.

Using the technique of mental noting with the breath can also help to stabilize the attention. You could use the note "In, out" if you feel the breath at the nose, or "Rise, fall" if you're sensing the movement of the chest or abdomen. Some of the Thai forest traditions use the word "Buddho" with each breath, one syllable on the in breath, the other on the out. Whatever word you use, it's important to keep it soft and light, so it doesn't interfere with the direct experience. You are not controlling the breath with your noting—the noting is simply a tool to maintain awareness of what is happening. As the meditation practice deepens, often the mental label falls away leaving only the bare awareness of the experience; but in the beginning of practice, the noting can be very helpful.

The breath serves as an anchor, a primary object of attention that we can return to again and again. This training of attention is found in most spiritual traditions. St. Francis of Sales, a French Catholic spiritual guide, expressed it very well: "If the heart wanders or is distracted, bring it back to the point quite gently. And even if you did nothing in the whole of your hour but bring your heart back, though it went away every time you brought it back, your hour would be very well employed."

It's helpful to remember that our effort is to be aware of just one breath at a time. Or perhaps even just half a breath. In the Buddha's words, "Breathing in, I know I'm breathing in; breathing out, I know I'm breathing out." It's very simple. But we often come to our meditation practice with an expectation that we should be able to be with the breath for most of the sitting. Then, when we find the mind wanders after just a breath or two, we become restless and discouraged. Being aware of just one half breath, though, is within our capacity. As we marshal our energy to be present for just half a breath, and then again, slowly the power of our concentration grows.

After sitting for some time, different sensations begin to arise in the body. At first, they may be uncomfortable feelings like pain, tension, tightness, heat, or pressure. At other times, more neutral or pleasant sensations come as well: vibration, tingling, softness, or lightness. Whenever a sensation becomes more predominant than the breath, let that sensation become the object of meditation, making a soft mental note to help keep the mind receptive and nonreactive. See if you can relax into the experience of it, letting it simply be there in the open space of awareness, in the same way you were with sounds. As you become mindful of this physical sensation, notice what happens to it in the process of observation. Does it grow stronger or weaker? Does it shift position or disappear? When it is no longer predominant, let your attention return to the breath.

Thoughts, images, and emotions also appear during meditation practice. As you are hearing sounds or following the breath, the mind begins to wander, getting lost in thought or fantasy. As soon as you become aware of the wandering mind, make a note of "Wandering," or "Thinking." What is the difference in your experience between being lost in thought and being aware that you're thinking? The moment of awakening from being lost should not be overlooked. Notice the clarity of awareness in that moment. If certain thought patterns become repetitive, make a specific note of the type of thought it is: "Judging," "Planning," "Remembering." Or if certain themes continually recur, you might label them "Family Tape," "Work Tape," "Vacation Tape," and so on. These notes help us unhook from the thoughts, so we can see them for what they are—empty phenomena rolling on.

The thought process is quite amazing. The very same phenomena that dominate our lives and actions when we're unaware of them are seen to be empty and transparent when we are aware. Dilgo Khyentse Rinpoche, one of the great Tibetan masters of the twentieth century, wrote, "Once we recognize that thoughts are empty, the mind will no longer have the power to deceive us. But as long as we take our deluded thoughts as real, they will continue to torment us mercilessly, as they have been doing throughout countless past lives."

For many people, vivid images arise during meditation practice. They may be remembered scenes, geometric forms, or imagined fantasies. In this particular practice of mindful awareness, we simply make the note "Seeing," and then notice what happens to the image as we observe it. Does it continue, fade, or vanish suddenly? The particular content of the image, although sometimes fascinating, is not important. When the thought or image disappears, we again return to awareness of the body, sounds, or the breath.

Different mind states and emotions also constitute an important part of our practice and of our lives. It is possible to feel them in the open clarity of awareness rather than drown in a sea of attachment to them. A wide range of emotions arise as we sit quietly in meditation: boredom, restlessness, agitation, calm, peace, interest, excitement, anger, irritation, love, compassion, desire, envy, jealousy, rage, depression, elation, kindness, equanimity, happiness. The list goes on and on. All these different mind states parade through our minds like small children coming to our door on Halloween, each in his or her own costume. Do we get taken in by the pirate or ghost or good fairy? Or do we see through the costume to the child underneath?

Our practice is to open to the whole range of moods and mind states, feeling the energy particular to each one, becoming aware of the experience in both body and mind, and letting them wash through, arising and passing like clouds in the sky. When anger arises, or love or joy, it is just anger angering, love loving, joy joying. Different feelings arise and pass, each simply expressing its own nature. Usually, though, we become caught up in the world of emotion, identifying with these feelings, thoughts, and sensations. When this occurs, we turn the flowing stream of impermanence into a rigid sense of separate self.

As an experiment in awareness, the next time you feel identified with a strong emotion or reaction or judgment, leave the story line and trace the physical sensation back to the energetic contraction, often felt at the heart center. It may be a sensation of tightness or pressure in the center of the chest. Then breathe and relax the heart, simply allowing the feelings and sensations to be there.

See if it is possible to be with emotions in the same open relaxed way you are with sounds. You might make a soft mental note of what the emotion is: "Anger," "Calm," "Interest," "Boredom," and so on, and notice as well the tone of the note. Is the tone itself nonjudgmental or reactive, accepting or rejecting? When we practice being mindful of these different feelings, two levels of understanding emerge. First, we can more easily nourish and cultivate the skillful states and simply let the unskillful ones go; and, second, we begin to see more and more clearly the insubstantial, empty nature of them all.

While we are paying close attention to the workings of our mind, purifying it as we strengthen awareness, another powerful factor to observe is intention. Intention, or volition, energizes the mind to effect an action, and it contains the power to bring about karmic results, much like a seed has the potential to germinate and grow. We often overlook the power of a seed, which seems so small. Yet when the conditions are right, a small acorn can become a huge oak tree. The motivations associated with each intention condition the results of the action that ensues. When kindness, generosity, love, and wisdom motivate our intentions, then happiness follows. When greed, anger, or delusion motivates our intentions to act, the result is suffering. The Buddha expressed this clearly in the famous first two verses of the *Dhammapada*:

> *Mind is the forerunner of all things.*
> *If one speaks or acts with an impure mind*
> *Suffering follows, like the wheel that follows the foot of the ox.*
>
> *Mind is the forerunner of all things.*
> *If one speaks or acts with a pure mind*
> *Happiness follows, like the shadow that never leaves.*

Because intention plays such a critical role in the unfolding of our lives, paying attention to it becomes a compelling interest. We begin this practice by noticing those obvious intentions that precede major movements of the body. Before you shift position, can you notice the intention in the mind to move? You may experience this as a particular thought, as some urge or impulse, or even as the simple knowing that you're about to move. I often refer to intention as the "about to" moment. We know we're about to do something before we do it. In times of moving more slowly and deliberately, awareness of intention becomes clear. As we become more practiced in this observation, intentions before other kinds of actions also become apparent.

This clarity of mind with respect to our intentions and motivations enables us to bring discriminating wisdom to our choices. When we are unaware, we simply act out the many habits of our conditioning. When we are aware, the same habitual impulses may arise, but we then have the choice to act or not act.

Once when I was on a retreat, a situation arose that reminded me again of the importance of noticing intention and motivation before acting. I was going through the lunch line at the Insight Meditation Society and noticed a sign in front of one of the dishes that said, "Moderation, Please." It happened that this request had been posted for a food I especially liked—sesame spinach. Just as I was about to take some, a quick thought arose in my mind, "I wonder how much I can have and still be moderate." I then proceeded to take as much as I felt I could get away with. About thirty seconds later, while still in line, I realized what had just happened—I had been carried away by a thought I hadn't seen clearly, and then been lost in an action. Although I was able to smile a bit at the workings of my own mind, the heap of spinach was already on my plate, and for the whole rest of the meal I kept looking back, somewhat guiltily, to see if everyone after me had had enough. If I had been a little more mindful of intention, I would have had a much more peaceful meal.

Another good place to practice this awareness is in the realm of speech. See if you can notice the intention to speak before the words actually come out. Just in that moment, can you bring to bear the wisdom of skillful speech and choose appropriately whether or not to voice that particular thought? You may soon find yourself enjoying more times of silence. Although at first this may seem an awkward exercise, with practice our mindfulness of all kinds of intentions becomes a natural part of our meditative life, with tremendous consequences for our happiness and well-being.

BARE ATTENTION

All of these instructions apply the perspective of bare attention to whatever experience arises. "Bare" here means simple, direct, noninterfering, and nonjudging. "Attention" refers to mindfulness, awareness, not forgetting. So bare attention is simple, direct, noninterfering awareness. Alert and relaxed, we're not looking for any experience in particular; we are simply awake to what presents itself. Observing in this way opens up worlds we may never have noticed.

Louis Agassiz was a Swiss-born American naturalist who helped train his students in careful observation. The following is a story told about Samuel Scudder, one of his students:

> [Agassiz] intended, he said, to teach the student to see—to observe and compare—and he intended to put the burden of study on them. Probably he never said what he is best known for: "Study nature, not books," or not in those exact words. But such certainly was the essence of his creed, and for his students the idea was firmly implanted by what they would refer to as "the incident of the fish."
>
> His initial interview at an end, Agassiz would ask the student when he would like to begin. If the answer was now, the student was immediately presented with a dead fish—usually a very long-dead, pickled, evil-smelling specimen, personally selected by the "master" from one of the wide-mouthed jars that lined his shelves. The fish was placed before the student in a tin pan. He was to look at the fish, the student was told, whereupon Agassiz would leave, not to return until later in the day, if at all.
>
> Samuel Scudder, one of the many from the school who would go on to do important work of their own (his in entomology), described the experience as one of life's memorable turning points.
>
> In ten minutes, I had seen all that could be seen in that fish. . . . Half an hour passed—an hour—another hour. The fish began to look loathsome. I turned it over and around: looked it in the face—ghastly; from behind, beneath, above, sideways, at three-quarters view—just as ghastly. I was in despair.

I might not use a magnifying glass; instruments of all kinds were interdicted. My two hands, my two eyes, and the fish; it seemed a most limited field. I pushed my finger down its throat to feel how sharp the teeth were. I began to count the scales in different rows until I was convinced that that was nonsense. At last, a happy thought struck me—I would draw the fish, and now with surprise, I began to discover new features in the creature.

When Agassiz returned later and listened to Scudder recount what he had observed, his only comment was that the young man must look again.

I was piqued; I was mortified. Still more of that wretched fish! But now I set myself to my task with a will, and discovered one new thing after another. . . . The afternoon passed quickly and toward its close, the professor inquired: "Do you see it yet?"

"No," I replied. "I am certain I do not. But I see how little I saw before."

The day following, having thought of the fish most of the night, Scudder had a brainstorm. The fish, he announced to Agassiz, had symmetrical sides with paired organs.

"Of course, of course," Agassiz said, obviously pleased. Scudder asked what he might do next, and Agassiz replied, "Oh, look at your fish!"

In Scudder's case, the lesson lasted a full three days. "Look, look, look," was the repeated injunction, and the best lesson he ever had, Scudder recalled, "a legacy the professor has left to me, as he has left it to many others, of inestimable value, which we could not buy, with which we cannot part."

Can we direct that intention, that power of observation, at our own minds? This is our life—can we look at it with that degree of care?

As awareness becomes steadier and concentration stronger, the quality of bare attention begins to reveal deeper insights into the world and into ourselves. We begin to cut through the stories we tell ourselves about experience, living less in thoughts about things and increasingly in the direct experience of the moment. As one example, we see that our experiences of past and future are simply thoughts in the moment, and so we become less caught up in them. St. Augustine once said, "If the past and future really exist, where are they?"

Notice the difference between being lost in some mind drama, and then recognizing it as just a thought. With that recognition, there is an instant sense of release, relaxation, and spaciousness. And instead of judging the fact that we were lost, we can delight in the experience of waking up. Often people misunderstand this point of practice, having the idea that meditation means never having any thoughts. The aim of practice, though, is not that; it is to be aware of thoughts, rather than to be lost in them. One of the founders of Korean Zen, the great master Chinul, said, "Don't be afraid of thoughts. Only take care lest your awareness of them be tardy." Of course, one of the consequences of this awareness is that we often see these thoughts quickly dissolve, precisely because we are not lost in them and thus unknowingly feeding them.

Directly understanding this difference between being lost in thoughts and being aware of them has a significant impact in our lives, because we are often not simply lost in thoughts, but also acting them out. So much of the suffering in the world—injustice, war, violence, and exploitation—comes from people acting out thoughts and feelings of greed, hatred, and fear. If we become aware of the greed or hatred or fear that is influencing us, we can then reflect upon that rather than strike out because of it. We need to see this root cause of suffering not only out there in other people's lives, but also in our own minds, our own lives as well.

Sometimes the simplest things are overlooked precisely because they are so simple. A profound aspect of bare attention is its natural capacity to include everything. When we are just being with what is, nothing falls outside the domain of awareness. A mirror doesn't choose what to reflect; its nature simply reflects whatever comes before it. Can we practice this same mirrorlike wisdom of mind?

During one of my stays at the monastery in Burma there was a huge amount of noise going on. Loudspeakers from the surrounding villages were playing music, women from neighboring houses were pounding their laundry on washing stones, and construction crews right outside my window were straightening steel rods, metal clanging on metal. There were times I just didn't believe what was going on. I went to my teacher, Sayadaw U Pandita, and told him about all this, expecting a little sympathy for the difficulty of my practice. All he said was, "Did you note it?" At first, I thought he was just trying to make the best of a bad situation. Later, I realized that he had pointed out a great truth.

In mindfulness practice, it doesn't matter at all what object arises; we can be as equally mindful and aware of noisy, abrasive sounds as of anything else. The empty, open, vividly clear nature of awareness is not altered by what appears. The recognition of this nature frees the mind from its habits of attachment and aversion.

This doesn't mean we should go looking for difficult situations or not try to create a quiet and peaceful atmosphere. But when unpleasantness of some kind is the truth of the situation, we can be with it with calm and equanimity. This doesn't mean becoming resigned to the unpleasantness, for resignation contains an element of aversion; rather, difficult or unpleasant experiences can point us back to the nature of awareness itself. The more we internalize the equality (from the perspective of mindfulness) of all objects, the more deeply we settle back into the Dharma's natural unfolding.

The teachings are simple, but they are not always easy. We quickly discover that, as with any great endeavor, they require energy, commitment, and perseverance. It's not the kind of effort that forces or expects things to happen. Rather, it's the effort to persevere through the innumerable ups and downs of the path. We need to keep going and to continually begin again.

COURAGE: STRENGTH OF HEART

The Pali word *viriya* is usually translated "effort," and it is considered the root of all achievement. But in our Western culture we can sometimes get out of balance by making too much effort. We may confuse *viriya* with ambitious striving or expectation; right effort then becomes overexertion, a straining quality of the mind. The Buddha pointed to this imbalance when he used the example of tuning the strings of a lute. A monk had been doing walking meditation with so much effort that his mind was becoming unsettled and agitated. The Buddha, knowing this monk had been a skilled musician earlier in his life, asked him what happened when the strings on his lute were too tight. The monk replied that the instrument was out of tune. Then the Buddha asked him about the strings being too loose, and he was given the same reply. In just the same way, the Buddha said, your effort "when overstrung, ends in agitation, when overlax, ends in sloth." The quality of our energy must be neither too tight nor too loose; then it can become the root of all achievement.

A less common translation of *viriya*, but one that highlights its essence for us in another way, is "courage." "Courage" comes from the root word for "heart" as being the seat of feeling and thought. It connotes spirit, vital force, and energy. It is the boldness and valor of mind that faces obstacles without shrinking from them. In the Pali texts, *viriya* is often used in opposition to sloth and torpor, that mind state commonly thought of as sleepiness, but that more deeply signifies retreating or withdrawing from difficulty. In this context too "courage" is an apt translation.

Some years ago, I was facing a situation of immense difficulty in my practice. For weeks, great pain and anguish permeated my experience. At the very lowest time, in a moment of hopeless despair, when any effort at all seemed impossible, the word "courage" suddenly appeared in my mind. It kept repeating, almost like a mantra, and each time the word sounded in my mind I could literally feel my heart grow stronger. With some magic of its own, it unhooked that last deep place of aversion and fear about what was happening that was keeping me separate from the experience. It brought forth the courage of simply being. What had been intolerable a moment before became completely acceptable. Courage is not about changing anything or grasping for some better state. It's the valor of truly being present.

Courage draws nourishment from patience, one of the perfections of the Buddha. Denis Saleh, a contemporary poet and author writes: "I have been hard at work now longer than I like to remember, on a novel set in Ancient Egypt. I found out how the Pyramids were built: *slowly*. Almost anything can be done, it seems, if one proceeds slowly enough, but we moderns simply cannot grasp this." There is tremendous wisdom in this statement: almost anything can be done if one proceeds slowly enough. Often we are discouraged by the enormity of a task or the length of a journey and become impatient with the difficulties we face. We lose faith in ourselves. Patience reminds us that what is in front of us is just this moment, just this step, just this breath. Patience, the Buddha said, leads to Nirvana.

As we deepen our meditation experience through mindfulness, courage, and patience, we begin to recognize the fruits of all our efforts. We are more awake, more alive, more joyful. An engaged interest starts to permeate our lives as we investigate aspects of ourselves that have gone unobserved for so long. What is a thought, that strange, ephemeral phenomenon that can so dominate our experience? What is an emotion, whose power sweeps over our minds and bodies? Who is knowing all of these things? What is the mind itself, this awareness, this power of consciousness? When we look for it, we don't find anything, and yet it continuously and effortlessly knows. This is a great mystery, which we can intimately touch with our understanding. Mindfulness is the key that unlocks the great dharma gates of all the Buddhist traditions.

EIGHT

LOVINGKINDNESS

*In the end, one suffuses the entire world with a mind of
lovingkindness, "vast, sublime, and immeasureable. . . ."*

—BHIKKHU BODHI

TWO OVERARCHING PRINCIPLES FRAME TWENTY-FIVE
hundred years of Buddhist wisdom and understanding. They provide a context for understanding many of the differences held so
dearly by different schools. Furthermore, they create a matrix for
seeing all of the varied teachings as part of the One Dharma of
freedom. These are the principles of relative and ultimate truth.
Relative truth is the world of our conventional reality. It is the
world of subject and object, self and other. All the familiar experiences of our lives are contained in this truth. *Ultimate truth* sees
the same world quite differently: no subject/object separation, in
fact, no "things" at all. Its very deepest aspect is the unmanifest,
the uncreated, the unborn, the undying.

As a way of understanding these two truths, think for a
moment of being in a movie theater, completely engrossed in the
story on the screen. We may feel happy or sad, excited or terri-
fied, all depending on the movie being shown. Now imagine

looking up at the beam of light that in passing through the film creates all of those images on the screen. As we sit in the darkened theater and see that light above us, we realize there is nothing really happening on the screen at all, except for a play of light and color. There is no one actually there falling in love or dying. And yet when we are absorbed in the story it feels very real. On the relative level, we live and act and relate as individuals, one with another, with all our personal stories and histories. On the ultimate level, there's no "self," no "I," no one there at all. It's all a play of momentary, changing elements. Moreover, what happens even to our perception of light when there's no screen, no dust particles in the air, no place for it to land?

One of the most illuminating stories illustrating the relative and ultimate levels is told about the death of His Holiness the Sixteenth Karmapa. (The Karmapa is the head of one of the four great lineages of Tibetan Buddhism). He had cancer and eventually died in a hospital in Zion, Illinois. In the last days of his illness, surrounded by his students and disciples who were saddened and concerned about the imminent death of their great teacher, he turned to them and said, "Don't worry, nothing happens."

This is quite an amazing understanding: on one level the body is sick and dying, and on another nothing happens. The union of these two truths, the relative and the ultimate, is the great mystery of our lives. We can easily get caught in attachment to either perspective. Sometimes we live so embroiled in the relative that our world becomes narrowly confined by the particular circumstances of our karma, whether pleasant or painful. Or we can be so attached to the ultimate, dismissing all experience as being empty, that we lose our connection with what the ancient Taoists called "the ten thousand joys and the ten thousand sorrows."

Over the years, different schools and traditions have emphasized one aspect or the other, sometimes dismissing the alternate perspective altogether. The path of One Dharma understands that each of these truths—the relative and the ultimate—*is* the expression of the other. And so we use whichever aspect, whichever means, is suitable for us at the moment. Sometimes relative practices prepare the ground for an understanding of the ultimate. At other times, our understanding of the ultimate informs our various practices on the relative level.

These two truths provide a context for understanding the newly emerging tradition of Western Buddhism. A beautiful example of this is in the spreading practice of lovingkindness, a practice the Buddha praised often as being a gateway to freedom. Lovingkindness (*metta* in Pali) is a quality of mind that is developed and expressed on the relative level of separate individuals, one being to another. And yet its highest manifestation comes from the understanding of emptiness, that there is no one ultimately there to be separate.

This practice is conducted quite differently in various Asian traditions, depending on which perspective is given emphasis. For example, in Zen practice there is almost no mention of lovingkindness meditation, although the very awakening of Zen brings people to an understanding of nonseparation. In the Theravada tradition of Southeast Asia, on the other hand, the *metta* chant is recited daily in many temples throughout the countryside.

Since these two traditions have come in contact with each other in the West, each has complemented aspects of the other. Some Zen practitioners are now incorporating *metta* meditation into their own practice, appreciating it on the relative level for the ease and spaciousness of mind it brings and, at the same time, understanding it on the ultimate level as the heart's expression of selflessness. And for meditators who embrace *metta* practice as a key element of relative truth, the Zen emphasis on the ultimate can bring about a transformed understanding of how they undertake this meditation. (This will become clear in later chapters as we discuss the "sudden awakening, gradual cultivation" of the great eleventh-century Korean Zen master Chinul.)

GENEROSITY OF THE HEART

Not only is lovingkindness an excellent example of how the path of One Dharma unites the different schools of Buddhism, it is also a key to the path itself. In this practice we can reclaim the potential for kindness—to ourselves and those around us.

What is this feeling of *metta* and why is it so honored in the teachings of early Buddhism? Sometimes in our lives we meet people who seem to radiate feelings of genuine love and kindness, people who seem to regard the whole world with loving care. They may be well-known people like Mother Teresa, Mahatma Gandhi, or Martin Luther King, Jr. Or they may be ordinary people we know who somehow have this great gift and capacity. When we're with people like this, they make us feel that at that moment we are the most important person in the world, not because of who we are or what we've done, but simply because we are a fellow living being.

This special quality of lovingkindness is the generosity and openness of heart that simply wishes all beings to be happy. *Metta* doesn't seek self-benefit; it's not offered with the expectation of getting something back. And because it's not dependent on external conditions, on people being or behaving in a certain way, it is not easily disappointed. As *metta* grows stronger, we feel more open to others, more open to ourselves, with benevolence and good humor. The poet W. H. Auden expressed it well: "Love your crooked neighbor with all your crooked heart."

Sometimes, as we practice sending feelings of lovingkindness to others, and ourselves, we may feel we are not loving enough. Or we expect *metta* to be an ecstatic feeling that will carry us away on waves of bliss, only then to feel discouraged when we don't feel particularly ecstatic. But lovingkindness can be better understood as the simple quality of friendly responsiveness to the people around us. More helpful translations of *metta* might be "good will" or a "kind heart." It is a basic openness of heart that allows the world in. When we look at ourselves and our actions in this way, we may find ourselves more loving than we think.

Like all qualities, *metta* can be strengthened through practice. The Buddha's great gift in teaching is that he leads us from wherever we are to the path of highest liberation. The opening lines of the *Metta Sutta*, the Buddha's discourse on lovingkindness, point out exactly how to prepare the ground for developing and deepening this kind of love: "In order to attain the state of peace one should be able, upright, straightforward, easy to speak to, gentle and not proud."

It's not enough to simply think love is a good idea. There's some work to be done, attention to be paid. We need to express it in the way we relate to people. Being able, upright, and straightforward means being committed to basic honesty and simplicity, so that we speak and act without deception or ulterior motives. Being easy to speak to and gentle means being approachable and actually making ease and gentleness our practice in the way we are with others. And not being proud reminds us of the true meaning of humility, which is not a stance of meekness, but rather the lack of self-centeredness. The writer Wei Wu Wei expressed this meaning with great insight: "True humility is the absence of anyone to be proud."

All of this requires practice. We need to notice those times when we are not being straightforward, gentle, or easy to speak to. And, on the other hand, we need to notice what happens when we let down the walls of defensiveness and fear, let go of the tension of separation, even for a few moments. Some time ago I was having a difficult conversation with a friend in which judgments, opinions, and undercurrents of ill will were flying back and forth. At some point I woke up to what was happening, took a few mindful breaths, and consciously relaxed the contraction I was feeling in my heart. In that moment of relaxing the heart and no longer being so identified with my own point of view, I opened to the experience of the space that held us both. And most strikingly, what characterized that space was the feeling of *metta*, of not being separate. Lovingkindness is accessible when we remember that it is.

The Buddha suggested other ways to strengthen this feeling. One method is to focus on the good qualities of others (and ourselves) rather than feeding the seductive habit of finding fault. It doesn't mean we are unaware of the difficult aspects of people— in fact, being aware of the whole picture keeps *metta* from becoming sentimental delusion. But by highlighting what is good, it becomes easier to abide in genuine good will, wishing well for all beings.

The Buddha also emphasized the development of gratitude, one of the most beautiful and rare qualities in the world. We so easily take for granted—or forget—the kindness people show us. Yet when we feel true gratitude, whether toward particular people or toward life, *metta* will flow from us naturally. When we connect with another person through gratitude, the barriers that separate begin to melt. Without "us" and "them," we are left simply in the openness of the situation, living in concord, just as those park-dwelling monks did in the time of the Buddha.

By focusing on what is good in ourselves and others and feeling gratitude for the good that people have done for us, we can more easily open to another quality of mind crucial to our happiness: forgiveness. Forgiveness means renouncing the suffering of anger and resentment. Abiding in a place where we no longer hold on to old grudges or hurts, we live in the present moment, undistracted by memories or projections. When we forgive another or ourselves, we remind ourselves that lovingkindness and happiness are possible. Our basic intention of good will is reflected in and expressed so well by these lines of the *Metta Sutta*: "May all beings be happy. Let none deceive another. Let none through anger or ill will wish harm upon another. Even as a mother protects with her life her only child, even so with a boundless heart should one cherish all living beings."

With these reflections in mind, we might begin each period of meditation with thoughts of forgiveness. "If I have hurt or harmed anyone in my thoughts or words or actions, I ask forgiveness. And I freely forgive anyone who may have hurt or harmed me." Sometimes this takes time to actualize, but even having the aspiration to forgive sets us on its path. The Dalai Lama put it very simply when he said, "Of course, there are moments when I do get angry, but in the depth of my heart, I don't hold a grudge against anyone."

Learning to live in a space of friendliness and love requires patience and constancy. Very often we fall back into familiar patterns of annoyance, irritation, anger, and ill will. But these states can also be a bell chime of mindfulness for us, reminding us to investigate rather than drown in them. Thomas Merton knew that going through difficult times is an essential part of the spiritual journey. He wrote, "Prayer and love are learned in the hour when prayer becomes impossible and the heart has turned to stone."

Working with Anger

How do we work with anger and aversion, when *metta* seems impossible and our heart has contracted? How can we investigate these unwholesome mind states that often are our habitual responses to unpleasant or difficult experiences? It's easy to observe them in our relationship to physical pain. There is often contraction, frustration, and impatience; we don't like it. We want the pain to go away, and we engage in all kinds of unproductive mental strategies to make it do so. We may get caught in waves of self-pity or lost in fear, or bargain with it in order to get it to leave: "I'll be mindful if you'll go away."

Or we may try to avoid discomfort in other ways. Years ago, when I was living and practicing in India, I went to Kashmir for some of the hot summer months. Part of the journey was a very long bus ride—many hours on a hot, crowded Indian bus. I had a cramped seat right over the crankshaft, and the bus rattled and vibrated all the way up the narrow mountain roads. I could see the ride was going to be really unpleasant, so I thought I would just stay with my breath for the whole time, keeping out all unpleasant sensations. One hour, two hours, noting the breath: "In, out, in, out."

For quite a while this strategy seemed to work. I became concentrated on the breath and wasn't too aware of the discomfort. But at a certain point, it just became too much effort. I was trying so hard to hold on to the breath and not feel anything else that I was getting exhausted from trying. At that point, there came a mini-awakening. I realized the real struggle was in trying to keep unpleasant things out and what I really needed to do was to let them in. From that moment's understanding, I simply began to open to whatever was arising—the heat, the noise, the uncomfortable feelings in the body, the vibrations, the smells from the engine, all of it. When I could let it all in, the mind relaxed, and the rest of the journey was fine. Things were just as they were; I no longer had to fight with them.

Aversion also arises when we remember certain unpleasant situations in the past or anticipate future ones. We can easily create scenarios in the mind that then make us angry or afraid. There's a story about an old Zen monk living in the mountains of Japan. He was a great artist, and he spent much of his time painting a tiger on the wall of his cave. After years of painstaking work creating a very realistic looking tiger, he finally finished the painting, looked at it, and became frightened. We are all too often frightened, angry, or upset at the painted tigers in our minds, at stories of past events or of an imaginary future.

Not being able to open to unpleasant emotions is another cause for anger and ill will to arise, further obscuring the possibility of *metta*. This often happens when we personalize a difficult situation that is, in fact, impersonal. Some years ago I was at the Newark airport on my way to Denver. We were on the plane, already taxiing out to the runway when the plane suddenly came to a stop. This didn't bode well. The pilot announced that because of high winds in Denver and the exceptionally heavy load on the plane, we needed to return to the gate and deplane about half the passengers—all those with connecting flights.

By the time we got back to the gate, one passenger was in great agitation about the delay and the possibility of being stranded overnight at the airport. He was shouting at the flight attendant, railing at the airlines, and generally venting a lot of anger. I was watching from my seat, and at first I felt a lot of antipathy for this person who was making such an unpleasant scene. But then I became interested in trying to understand what was really going on.

It was clear that the situation in itself was frustrating. Long delays, needing to change all kinds of arrangements—I think most of us were having the same feelings of distress. But this particular person was unable to hold the frustration and be with it in a somewhat balanced way. The frustration itself was so unpleasant for him, even intolerable, that it rebounded into anger. Clearly, the flight attendant had nothing to do with the decision; in fact, the decision itself was based on safety considerations. It certainly was not a personal vendetta against the passengers by the airline, although in situations like this it often feels like it is. This incident was a striking example for me of the great power of mindfulness to alleviate suffering. If the passenger had been able to take a breath or two, to open to the feelings of distress, and perhaps think about how he would have wanted to be treated as an airline employee in such a situation, he might not have lashed out as he did. When we can be with unpleasant emotions as well as difficult physical sensations, this acceptance begins to free us from the habit of aversive reactions and lets us rest in a place of ease.

In all forms of aversion the heart contracts. We then become imprisoned by our own mind's reactions and subsequently solidify a sense of self and separation. But there is also something extremely seductive about anger that keeps pulling us in and feeding it. The Buddha described it well when he said, "Anger, with its poisoned root and honeyed tip." We feel empowered, energetic, and often self-righteous when we're lost in angry feelings. We may feel it gives us the energy necessary to take appropriate actions.

There is, however, a much deeper and more skillful source of power, one that is not poisoned and so does not bring any harmful results. That is the power of love and compassion. We can practice having *metta* not only for other persons—even when they are being difficult—but also for the anger itself, for our own suffering minds. Thich Nhat Hanh, the wonderful Vietnamese meditation master, poet, and peace activist, suggested that when we are feeling anger we should hold it in our arms with great tenderness. He said that bringing mindfulness to the anger is like the sun shining on a flower; the flower cannot resist opening when the sunshine penetrates it. Likewise, when we hold the anger with love and compassion, it opens and reveals its depth and roots.

As we practice lovingkindness it sometimes seems as if we have even more aversion than when we started, that we are getting more irritable. But if we can stay mindful of what's happening, there is a powerful purifying process going on. It's as if cool drops of water are falling on a piece of red-hot metal. As each drop hits the metal there is the sound of steam rising. Over and over again, the cool water hits the hot metal . . . "whoosh." But gradually the sound of steam rising from the drops diminishes until there is no reaction at all. The metal has cooled off. Our minds work in a similar way. We all carry a vast storehouse of impressions, old reactions, judgments, and hurts. As we begin practicing loving wishes, these often come to the surface . . . "whoosh." But over time, these reactive patterns begin to lose strength and we find ourselves living with greater ease and happiness and joy.

The following is an account of the Zen master Ryokan by Tekiken, the adopted son of one of Ryokan's students. It illustrates the wonderful union of the relative and absolute levels in the openheartedness of loving feeling:

When the Zen Master went out, children would follow him. Sometimes they would shout at him loudly, and the Master would shout back in surprise, throwing up his hands, reeling backward and almost losing his balance. Whenever the children found the Master, they were always ready to do this. Ordinary people frowned on this behavior. My late father once questioned the Master about it. The Master laughed and told him: "When the children are happy, it makes *me* happy. The children are happy, and I'm happy too, everyone is happy together, and so I do it all the time. There's no truer happiness than this!" This happiness of the Master's was itself a manifestation of the ultimate truth.

NINE

COMPASSION

Beings are numberless, I vow to save them.
Delusions are inexhaustible, I vow to end them.
Dharmagates are boundless, I vow to enter them.
Buddha's way is unsurpassable, I vow to become it.

—THE FOUR BODHISATTVA VOWS
(SAN FRANCISCO ZEN CENTER)

THE BODHISATTVA VOWS ABOVE EMBODY THE ALTRUISTIC
view that our motivation for practice is not just to enlighten
ourselves, but for the awakening of all beings. Raising this bodhisattva ideal to a central place of aspiration marked one of the
great dividing lines between the Theravada tradition and the
later developments of Mahayana Buddhism.

What exactly were the issues involved? And are they still
relevant today? The historical development that played itself
out in the centuries following the Buddha's life revolves
around a basic question that is at the heart of all spiritual
undertaking. Do we purify ourselves first, so that we can then
take care of others? Or is it by taking care of others that we
purify ourselves? Arhants or bodhisattvas? And is there an

understanding in One Dharma that somehow unifies both perspectives?

Going back again to the time of the Buddha, in those early years after his enlightenment there was very little reference to a bodhisattva path. Of course, the Buddha himself was an exemplar of it, but it was understood that Buddhas appeared only once in a very long while—in fact, there were many aeons between them (an aeon being the time it would take to wear down a mountain if once every hundred years a bird brushed its peak with a silk scarf)—and that when Buddhas did appear they taught a more expedited path to freedom, that is, the attainment of arhantship. This attainment is the mind that is free of all defilement, free of all suffering, and, according to Theravada theory, the end of rebirth.

The Buddha was explicit about the compassionate activity following such realization. Early in his teaching, when the first sixty of his disciples had become arhants, he exhorted them in this way:

> Go forth, O Bhikkhus, for the good of the many, for the happiness of the many, out of compassion for the world, for the good, benefit and happiness of people and devas [celestial beings]. Let not two go by one way. Teach the Dhamma, excellent in the beginning, excellent in the middle, excellent in the end. Proclaim the noble life, altogether perfect and pure. Work for the good of others, you have done your duties.

But after the Buddha's death and the later split of the Second Council, the monks of the Great Assembly began emphasizing the way of the bodhisattva, first as a viable path for a few and later even as a preferred ideal for everyone. Gradually, teachings about the *paramitas* appeared. These are the perfections a bodhisattva needs to become a fully enlightened Buddha, the qualities of generosity, virtue, patience, energy, meditation, and wisdom. Of course, these qualities were mentioned individually in the Sutras, but they had not previously been explicitly formulated as part of a path to Buddhahood.

Teaching the perfections also served to include the laity in the path of spiritual development. Just as the bodhisattva brought these spiritual qualities to perfection, so too could any individual slowly develop them over many lifetimes. The schools developing from the Great Assembly began introducing the perfections through the Jataka tales, the appealing stories of the Buddha in his past lives, when he took both human and animal births, gradually refining the perfection of his character. The *paramitas* also began to be included in the more formalized lists of accepted teachings. At this stage, all the schools honored the path of the bodhisattva, but they still held it to be for those few exceptional individuals who had the strength of determination and character to persevere over the aeons of time necessary to become a Buddha.

It was only in the full flowering of Mahayana, in the period from 100 B.C.E. to 300 C.E., that Buddhahood was articulated as the universal final goal for everyone. A famous parable from the Mahayana *Lotus Sutra* explains this new vision of Buddhahood. The Sutra describes children playing in a burning house, heedless of the fire and the danger they are in. A fully awakened Buddha is likened to a loving father who, out of great compassion for his children, finds different ways to lure them out of the house. Some he promises a little goat cart, others something grander, depending on their interests and desires. But when they have all escaped to safety, he gives them all the best and highest of what he has. In this simile, the Buddha entices some people to practice by the thought of ending their own suffering, the arhant ideal; he entices others by the thought of saving all beings, the bodhisattva path. But from the new Mahayana perspective, no matter what the initial motivation is, all will eventually reach the highest goal of Buddhahood.

Two questions emerge. The first is whether the aspiration for Buddhahood is indeed a realistic one for all beings. Do we all really have the immense fortitude necessary to become a Buddha, when becoming an arhant—no little accomplishment—is a relatively quicker route to freedom?

The second question, which may illuminate the first, is whether the various traditions are actually using the term "Buddha" in the same way. For example, when great masters in both the Tibetan and Zen traditions (and perhaps others as well) are spoken of as "living Buddhas," what does this mean? Have they attained the same perfections of mind as the historical Buddha, Siddhartha Gautama? Was their experience of awakening identical? Or might it mean that their freedom of mind is the same, that the compassionate motivation to benefit all beings is the same, but that they don't necessarily have the same range of power and skillful means?

We can look at this question of Buddha terminology in a historical context. The Mahayana Sutras extolling Buddhahood and the bodhisattva path were written in part as a counterpoint to the growing scholasticism of the earlier schools, represented in the Mahayana view by the arhant ideal and the Abhidharma philosophy. And the later Zen teachings of a direct transmission outside of the texts was, in turn, a move away from the philosophic debates and outwardly directed devotional practices of some Mahayana teachings.

In both of these cases, at different times in history, pointing to "the Buddha Mind within" was a potent reminder that the Buddha—awakening—is not to be found outside of ourselves. This is the use of language as skillful means. Words used in radically new ways have the power to free us from limiting preconceptions. Hui Neng, the Sixth Zen Ancestor and one of the most influential figures of Buddhism in China and later Japan, writes:

We should work for Buddhahood within the essence of mind.
We should not look for it apart from ourselves. He who is kept
in ignorance of his essence of mind is an ordinary being. He who
is enlightened in his essence of mind is a Buddha.

So when we are encouraged to take the bodhisattva vow to become Buddha, in order to liberate all beings, what kind of Buddha do we have in mind? Gautama Buddha? Hui Neng Buddha? Are we striving for the full perfection and all the unique powers of Buddhahood, or are we aiming for the enlightenment of understanding the essence of our minds with the compassionate resolve to help others?

A radical notion is that perhaps many of the great Mahayana masters were indeed arhants, in its earliest meaning of being fully liberated, but because of the Mahayana literature that demeaned arhants, they no longer thought in, or used, that term. There might have been less difference in experience than there was in terminology.

As the different traditions are now meeting in the West, is it possible to hold these various perspectives—bodhisattva versus arhant—without creating an irresolvable sectarian conflict of views? Is there a way they can inform, rather than oppose, one another? Issues in my own practice highlighted this problem. From my earliest introduction to Buddhism, I had read of the bodhisattva vows and been inspired by them. But at the same time, given my own conditioning and limitations, I felt they were far beyond my capacity to undertake. As much as I would like to save all beings, how could I ever conceivably do so? Was it even possible? And so I continued my meditation practice, just trusting that as I became less selfish, more kind, and more generous, it would inevitably benefit those around me, even without my taking a formal vow to help them.

Our dharma practice cannot help but benefit the world. As our minds become purified of those forces that create suffering, the habits of greed and hatred and ignorance, the world is that much freer of the many consequences of those mind states. But what would it take to go from the understanding that our practice will inevitably help others to making the welfare of others the very motivation to practice? Knowing our own limitations, can we realistically put this altruistic motivation right at the beginning? And what would be the effect of doing so?

A great turning point for me in opening to this possibility occurred at the Dzogchen retreat mentioned earlier. Nyoshul Khen Rinpoche was giving teachings on relative and ultimate *bodhicitta*. *Bodhicitta* literally means "awakened heart." On the relative level it is compassion, expressed in the bodhisattva vow to save all beings; it is the aspiration to awaken from ignorance in order to live one's life for the benefit of all. On the ultimate level, *bodhicitta* goes beyond the concepts of self and other. It is the empty, aware nature of the mind itself. As Rinpoche was teaching about these two aspects—compassion and emptiness—there was an unexpected moment of insight as I realized that the relative level *is* the expression of the ultimate: compassion *is* the activity of emptiness. Suddenly the great and seemingly impossible burden of "someone" (me!) having to save all beings dissolved into the great expansive arena of selfless compassionate action. Compassionate action is the natural responsiveness of awareness free of self: no one there "doing" anything.

In his teaching about the man (or woman) of no reliance, the ninth-century Chinese Zen master Rinzai expressed the creativity and unlimited potential of a person not imprisoned by the notion of self:

> If a man comes to me asking for the Buddha, as a man of no reliance, I present myself in a state of purity and cleanliness. If he asks for a bodhisattva, I present myself in a state of mercy and benevolence. If he asks for Bodhi—true wisdom—I present myself in a state of purity and exquisite superbness. If he asks for Nirvana—complete enlightenment—I present myself in a state of utter serenity. Though there are hundreds of thousands of states, as a man of nonreliance, I am always the same. Therefore, my presentation of various states according to the requirements is just like the Moon that freely presents its images on every surface of water.

Here, then, is where relative and ultimate *bodhicitta*—compassion and emptiness—merge, becoming expressions of each other. The more we practice the compassionate responsiveness of relative *bodhicitta*, the more easily we recognize the selfless quality of the mind's essence. And the more we recognize the innate empty wakefulness of the mind's essential nature, the more spontaneously compassionate we are in all situations.

When we let go of needing answers to the unknowable—just what *is* the Buddha's mind like?—we can simply take refuge in the basic and boundless principles of wisdom and compassion. We all recognize the need to purify our own minds. And the seemingly different points of view sit in harmony if we undertake this purification with the compassionate motivation that our own awakening be for the benefit and welfare of all. Then, whatever kind of Buddhahood we aspire to, we are actually taking steps on the path.

RELATIVE BODHICITTA IS COMPASSION

Relative *bodhicitta* (a term used in the Tibetan tradition) is the practice of compassion and compassionate action. Compassion is the strong and deep feeling that wants to alleviate the suffering of beings, and it arises when we allow ourselves to come close to suffering, both our own and that of others. This is a profound and difficult practice. We may want to be compassionate, and even feel that we often are, but it is not always easy to do. Just as we don't like to be with our own pain, we don't necessarily want to be with the pain of others. Strong tendencies of the mind often keep us defensive or indifferent or apathetic in the face of suffering.

As an experiment, watch your mind the next time you come close to a situation of suffering, either in others or yourself. What happens? Do you feel uneasy, withdraw, deny it, or let it in? Some years ago a friend of mine was in the hospital for some surgery. In trying to insert the needle for the IV, the doctor had a hard time finding the vein and so the process took quite a while. My friend was in considerable distress. The doctor's only response was, "What's wrong? It doesn't hurt." When we're not able to be present for the suffering that is right before us, this caps the wellspring of compassion within us.

In her poem "Beyond the Snow Belt," Mary Oliver writes of a storm taking lives not far from where we live, yet

> . . . except as we have loved,
> All news arrives as from a distant land.

The question for us, then, is how can our hearts stay open given the magnitude of suffering that exists in the world? We are bombarded with so many reports from distant lands—or even from the neighboring state—cataloguing the range of human distress. Is it even possible to open to it all with compassion?

For some of us, compassion may be at the very heart of what we aspire to in our lives. As an expression of his enlightenment, the Buddha is often known as the Great Compassionate One. But care is needed as we explore the meanings, nuances, and also possible hidden pitfalls of this practice. The word "compassion" contains and expresses feelings of openness, caring, and inter-connectedness that we would be hard put to quarrel with. It is possible, though, to sentimentalize and idealize these feelings, and then become content simply with the idea of compassion. Or we may judge ourselves for not having enough of it, or maybe take a subtle pride in our more compassionate moments.

In cultivating compassion, we need to start with ourselves and those closest to us. We practice opening, in meditation and in our lives, to difficulties that are present, right now, right here. It may be our own physical or emotional pain; or it may be the suffering of an agitated person sitting next to us on his meditation cushion, or on the subway, or in her car stuck in traffic on the freeway. The practice of meditation is learning to let things in, being with them as they are, without drowning in the difficulties or becoming identified with them. The great lesson here is that it is not what is happening that is important, but rather how we are relating to it. As we learn to open and come close to the suffering in our own lives, we find we have greater strength and courage and insight to be with the suffering of others. This is the great gift of mindfulness to compassion.

At first, as we undertake the cultivation of compassion, we may feel genuine empathy with others in pain or difficulty. This happens when we take the time to stop and feel what is really going on—even for just a few moments before rushing on with our lives. When we ask someone, "How are you?" do we really give him or her the gift of our attention? In situations in which people are behaving badly do we stop to look and feel what may be going on underneath, with our focus on easing the suffering rather than reacting to the behavior?

But compassion is also something more than these moments of empathy. It is not simply a feeling for the pain of others—it also contains within it a strong motivation to act. Thich Nhat Hanh expressed this perfectly when he said, "*Compassion is a verb.*" As we develop the relative aspect of *bodhicitta*, compassionate action, we begin to practice an active engagement with suffering in the world, responding to the various needs of beings in whatever way is appropriate and possible.

There are many examples of people who are open to the suffering that is present and then act to alleviate it. It may be in small, perhaps unregarded ways—simply being kinder, more generous, or more forgiving of the people around us. It may be giving a gift to someone in our lives we find difficult.

Some time ago a friend was on a lovingkindness and compassion retreat at the Insight Meditation Society. As he was going for a walk one day, he passed a neighbor shoveling snow in front of his home. This particular neighbor had a rough demeanor and in the past had voiced many angry words to others, myself included. For the most part, I just tried to avoid him. But this friend, not having any of my preconceptions, stopped and chatted a bit, commenting on the several feet of snow that had fallen in the last storm and how much shoveling there was to do. The neighbor replied gruffly that it was indeed a lot, especially with his bad heart. My friend then continued on, but after a few steps stopped, realized what the man had just said, and went back to shovel out his path. It was an obvious and compassionate thing to do, but to see it and do it took being open to the situation, free of projections. The neighbor then invited him inside for some hot drinks, and they talked for an hour or more.

At other times, compassion finds expression in acts of tremendous courage and determination in the face of hardship, difficulty, and danger. As just one example of many, Martin Luther King, Jr., who led nonviolent marches in the midst of flaring hatred, embodies the understanding from many spiritual traditions and expressed in the *Dhammapada* that "Hatred never ceases by hatred; it only ceases by love. This is a timeless truth." Compassion for the suffering of the oppressed, compassion for the suffering of the oppressor—it's not an easy task to have the heart hold both. The Dalai Lama speaks of how our enemies teach us patience: a potent reminder that even in the most difficult of circumstances we can develop our capacity for love.

In the summer of 1989, a Harvard medical journal published an article about a Tibetan doctor named Tendzin Choedrak, who had been a personal physician to the Dalai Lama. Imprisoned in 1959, Dr. Choedrak was held by the Chinese for the next twenty-one years. As he described it, for seventeen of those twenty-one years he was beaten and tortured daily, both physically and psychologically. His life was under daily threat. In the medical journal article he described four points of understanding that made possible not only his survival—because people survive very horrendous conditions in many ways—but also the fact that he survived psychologically and spiritually intact, with a heart that remained open to love and did not close down in anger and fear.

Dr. Choedrak's first insight was to see his situation in a larger context. He saw that even in the most deplorable human circumstances some human greatness could be accomplished, that in the face of great suffering and injustice he could practice love. What a reminder for us as we bring this perspective to our own lives, even in much less trying circumstances.

His second understanding was that his enemies, his torturers, were human beings like himself. He did not forget the commonality of the human condition and the laws that govern it. The law of karma means that all actions have consequences for the people who perform them, and Dr. Choedrak knew deeply that those people who were being so cruel to him were actually in adverse circumstances, just as he was. They were creating the karma that would bring their own future suffering. And rather than reflecting on the law of karma as a vehicle for revenge, Dr. Choedrak understood karma as a vehicle for compassion. This is the wisdom that unites us.

The third insight that helped him was his understanding of the need to let go of pride and self-importance. He actually attributed his very survival to this ability to let go of self-righteousness, even when it might have felt so justified. Letting go of these feelings is an indispensable practice on our spiritual journey.

The fourth of his insights that allowed him to triumph in his situation was the understanding that hatred, anger, and ill will never cease if we react with the same kind of feelings. They cease only in response to love. Love and compassion grow when we see that there are really no viable alternatives. The Buddha demonstrated this understanding in his unwavering motivation over countless lifetimes not only to alleviate the suffering of particular situations, but also to uncover the very root causes of suffering in our lives.

Although it is a powerful force on its own, compassion is greatly enhanced when it is balanced by wisdom, by the power of clear seeing, so that the actions we take are meaningful and effective. When compassion and wisdom are both present, they bring a certain magic and power to the world. They help us to see beyond the ordinary conventions and come out of the confinement of habituated response. Compassion directed by wisdom can take many forms. Sometimes it is soft and gentle, and sometimes forceful, decisive actions are needed. The Buddha himself did not shy away from such courses of action.

There is a story of a monk named Channa, who had been Prince Siddhartha's charioteer and friend before Siddhartha became the Buddha. Presuming on his former friendship with the young prince, Channa was quite lax in the monastic discipline. He was frequently admonished, but to no avail. Then, in one of the last actions before he died, the Buddha directed that none of the other monks or nuns speak or associate with Channa in any way. A short time afterward, the Buddha passed away. At this point, Channa became so dismayed and ashamed that this had been one of the Buddha's last acts, he became motivated to practice the Dharma with courageous energy and perseverance. And, as the story goes, before long, Channa too became one of the arhants, the enlightened ones.

There is no hierarchy of compassionate action. There is no particular prescription for what we should do. The field of compassion is limitless. In all of the traditions, people undertake a great range of activity in order to help others. In fact, some schools are characterized by "crazy wisdom," those actions that look askance at custom, but serve the higher motivation of helping suffering beings. We each find our own way. It can take the form of active engagement with the world; it can take the form of living in a cave in the Himalayas. Pascal, the famous seventeenth-century philosopher and mathematician, once wrote, "Most of the problems of the world would be solved if people could learn to sit quietly in a room."

If we cultivate the seeds of *bodhicitta*—"May my life and practice be for the benefit of all"—or even have the aspiration to have this motivation, slowly the seeds germinate and take root in our lives. Henry David Thoreau expressed this well: "Though

I do not believe that a plant will spring up where no seed has been, I have great faith in a seed. Convince me that you have a seed there, and I am prepared to expect wonders."

PRACTICING BODHICITTA

How can we actually practice the aspiration of *bodhicitta*, the motivation to awaken for the benefit of all beings? We can approach it from two sides. One side is highlighted in the Pali texts of Theravada Buddhism, where the Buddha emphasized that by truly taking care of ourselves, that is, by purifying our own minds and hearts, we naturally and inevitably take care of others. It is like two people being stuck in a muddy river bottom. If they try to help each other out of the muck, they may well both continue to founder. But if one of them first reaches solid ground, then he or she can easily help the other to safety.

We hear this basic principle in the safety guidelines of every airline. "If there is a sudden loss of cabin pressure the oxygen masks will appear. Please put on your own mask first and then assist those around you." If we try to help others before we are able to, it can lead to difficulties for all. But as we purify our own hearts and minds we find the "solid ground of emptiness"; we automatically become less self-centered. As there is less greed, less fear, less ignorance in our minds, we naturally live with more kindness and compassion.

The Indian sage Shantideva, in his famous work *The Way of the Bodhisattva* expressed the second way we can develop *bodhicitta*. This approach develops compassionate action—the aspiration to benefit all beings—by the practice of putting others before oneself, by thinking of others as being more important than oneself. When we give more importance to others, the strength of self-concern diminishes. The Dalai Lama is a great devotee of Shantideva and is a shining example of the fruits of this practice.

Contained within Shantideva's great masterpiece are verses that encapsulate this aspect of *bodhicitta*:

For all those ailing in the world,
Until their every sickness has been healed,
May I myself become for them
The doctor, nurse, the medicine itself.

Raining down a flood of food and drink,
May I dispel the ills of thirst and famine.
And in the ages marked by scarcity and want,
May I myself appear as drink and sustenance.

For sentient beings, poor and destitute,
May I become a treasure ever-plentiful,
And lie before them closely in their reach,
A varied source of all that they might need.

My body, thus, and all my goods besides,
And all my merits gained and to be gained,
I give them all away withholding nothing
To bring about the benefit of beings.

Like the earth and the pervading elements,
Enduring like the sky itself endures,
For boundless multitudes of living beings,
May I be their ground and sustenance.

Thus for everything that lives,
As far as are the limits of the sky,
May I provide their livelihood and nourishment
Until they pass beyond the bonds of suffering.

It's possible to read this and become inspired by its great generosity of spirit, but we may also feel a little overwhelmed. Would we ever be able to fulfill such an aspiration, given that our motives are often mixed, or hidden, or a series of conflicting ones?

Some time ago I was on a retreat and I came across a story in the Buddhist texts that I thought a colleague of mine would like to have in a book she was writing. Of course, among dharma teachers, a new story is worth quite a lot, and we often vie to lay claim to one. Well, I came across this text and my first thought was, "This will be a good story for my friend." But then, immediately following, came the thought, "No, I think I'll keep it for myself." Then, "No, I'll give it to her, and that way more stories will come back to me." Then I reflected, "That's just being selfish. It's better just to tell her what the story is. But maybe when I tell her, I'll also mention everything I'm going through," feeling a little pride in my sacrifice and half unconsciously wanting to put her in my debt. As my mind went through this run of thoughts and feelings, it made me wonder where in the midst of all this thinking was the purity of motivation simply to give? Then I realized that it was there, right in the first moment's thought to offer the story. And even though my mind entertained all these other thoughts and feelings and motives, I could always come back to that first moment of pure motivation. The postscript to all of this is that when I finally showed my friend this story from the texts, she didn't even want to use it.

So when the jumble of our thoughts and feelings confuses us, when we feel we are unable to act from a totally clear heart, perhaps we can follow the Dalai Lama's lead when he said, "I cannot pretend to practice *bodhicitta*, but deep inside me I realize how valuable and beneficial it is. That is all."

Rather than solidifying and then polarizing these two approaches to *bodhicitta*, as happens in sectarian attachments, we can see them as two sides of the same principle, helping to balance out the dangers that may arise from each one by itself. If we overemphasize our own purification at the expense of helping others, our spiritual journey may become narrow and self-absorbed. Likewise, if we always put others before ourselves, we may fall into patterns of confused codependence in which we ignore our own welfare simply to please others. So, from one side, we do the work of purifying ourselves, but with the motivation that it be for the welfare and benefit of all. And from the other side, even as we practice putting others before ourselves, we understand this as being part of our own path of purification. This unification is the path of One Dharma.

We plant this wonderful seed of relative *bodhicitta*, the kind heart, and slowly it will grow and mature into the guiding principle of our lives. Even at those times when we're not acting from this place of wisdom and compassion, *bodhicitta* can still be the reference point that reminds us of other choices. One Tibetan teaching sums up the power of this practice: "Let those who desire Buddhahood not train in many dharmas—but only one. Which one? Great compassion. Those with great compassion possess all the Buddha's teaching as if it were in the palm of their hand."

TEN

LIBERATION THROUGH NONCLINGING

Live in the nowhere that you come from,
Even though you have an address here.

—RUMI

A GREAT VISION FLOWS FROM THE BUDDHA'S ENLIGHTEN-
ment: beings wandering over countless lifetimes through different
realms of existence, innumerable world systems, unimaginable
immensities of time, and, at the heart of it all, the possibility of
awakening. Although we may have some growing confidence in
the teachings of the Buddha, for most of us certain aspects of this
cosmology remain outside the realm of our direct experience.
Not many of us have experienced space travel through other
realms. However, there is another way of understanding the
vastness and depth of this dharma journey—that is, opening to
the mystery of consciousness itself, to the fundamental nature of
our own minds, and to seeing what it is that binds us and what it
is that frees us.

What Is Consciousness?

Consciousness is the knowing faculty of the mind. "Knowing" does not refer to knowledge we acquire about something, like learning to drive a car or taking a course in chemistry, but rather to the immediate direct cognizing of the object itself—knowing a sight, a sound, a thought. We may hear a sound and then think "bird." The first moments of consciousness would be the knowing of the sound, followed then by moments of knowing the thought. Moments of consciousness are often clouded by the mental factor of delusion, which is characterized by fixation, contraction, attachment, or resistance—not seeing things as they are. We call this delusion of mind "ignorance." Sometimes consciousness is free of attachment and clinging, free of delusion. I call this wisdom mind "awareness."

Most of us are familiar with experiences of the mind being clouded by ignorance. It is when we are caught up in wanting, attachment, fear, or aversion, when we are lost in thoughts of past and future. It's as if our experiences of sensations, thoughts, and emotions arise with Velcro loops, and delusion is the Velcro hook; when delusion is present we stick. The Buddha used many terms to describe these states of delusion: hindrances, defilements, floods, taints, bonds, and fetters. It is important to notice the contraction of mind when these deluded states are present, because each of these moments is really a moment of suffering.

In talking of the hindrances, the Buddha said: "When these five hindrances are unabandoned in himself, a bhikkhu sees them respectively as a debt, a disease, a prisonhouse, slavery, and a road across a desert. But when these five hindrances have been abandoned in himself, he sees that as freedom from debt, healthiness, release from prison, freedom from slavery, and a land of safety." These metaphors are not simply philosophical concepts; they actually reflect the feeling of the mind contracted in ignorance or released in wisdom.

Although delusion is a strong habit, the good news is that it is not intrinsic to the mind itself. All of the defilements of mind are visitors. They may come frequently, but there are also moments free of delusion. It's helpful to understand and recognize these moments, because the more clearly we recognize the wisdom mind, the easier it is to return to it.

LIBERATION THROUGH NONCLINGING

There are many different descriptions of awakening, but all Buddhist traditions converge in one understanding of what liberates the mind. The Buddha expressed it clearly and unequivocally: "Nothing whatsoever is to be clung to as 'I' or 'mine.' Whoever has heard this truth has heard all the Teachings, whoever practices this truth has practiced all the Teachings, whoever has realized this Truth has realized all the Teachings." This is the essential unifying experience of freedom—the heart of the One Dharma of liberation. *Nothing whatsoever is to be clung to as "I" or "mine."*

Centuries later, the great Indian Vajrayana adept Tilopa gave the same teaching to his disciple Naropa. "Naropa, you are not fettered by appearances, you are fettered by attachments. So cut your attachments." And much more recently, a meditator I know expressed this truth when he said, "Suffering is rope burn." Suffering comes from trying to hold on as the rope is inexorably pulled through our hands. Our unfolding experience keeps changing—sometimes it is pleasant, sometimes unpleasant—but the practice of freedom is always the same, namely, liberation through nonclinging.

We're not practicing in order to have some better experience, however nice or wonderful it may be. We're practicing what the Buddha called the heart's release. As a further help to us, in case we're not exactly sure where we tend to grasp, the Buddha pointed out the major arenas of attachment, in both our meditation and our lives. We can investigate these in our minds, learn how to let them go, and thus practice the mind of freedom.

ATTACHMENT TO SENSE PLEASURES

We habitually cling to the pleasure of sense objects. It may be pleasant bodily sensations or pleasant thoughts or feelings, something we don't want to let go of. This attachment to pleasant feelings reveals a lot about the power of addiction, fascination, and enchantment. The Dalai Lama told a story about this at a conference in Los Angeles. It seems that each morning on his way to the meetings he drove past a long line of shops selling the latest high-tech gadgets. At first, he just looked with interest at the different things in the windows as he passed by. But, he said laughing, by the end of the week he found himself wanting things even though he didn't know what they were.

An image that has helped me notice the allure of pleasant feeling in meditation is that of driving along on a freeway and seeing an exit sign for some attraction—whatever the particular enjoyment of the moment may be. Then my mind takes that particular exit and spends time in the amusement park, until I finally notice what is going on. At that point, I get back on the freeway of mindfulness again. Some time later, another sign appears, equally seductive. I still get off at the exit, but this time I realize what's happening more quickly and get right back on the highway. When my mind is quite alert, I see the signs by the side of the road, and I'm able to simply note "Seeing" as I pass them by, without breaking the rhythm or continuity of awareness at all.

In addition to pleasant sensory experiences, we can also start clinging to pleasant meditation experiences, feelings of great rapture, calm, happiness, and peace. At these times a teacher can be very helpful. During one period of practice with Sayadaw U Pandita, my meditation was going quite smoothly, and each day I would report more and more refined details of what was happening. Usually Sayadaw was quite pleased to hear such reports. But in this particular instance, as I was describing the minutest details, he looked at me and said, "You're attached to subtlety."

We can also get lost in a compelling fascination with the unfolding process itself. It's as if we are leaning into the next moment, leaning into the flow of phenomena, as if somehow the next breath, the next moment will provide resolution. We are then caught in the "in-order-to mind," where we attend to one experience in order to have the next. Freedom is found not in some particular new experience, but in the mind of no clinging, where the gears of attachment are disengaged. Another "mantra" that can remind us of the possibility of freedom now is: *"It doesn't matter to what we don't cling."* We don't have to wait for a special experience in order not to cling. We can practice freedom right now. This doesn't mean we close off to feelings and experience. The mind of no clinging is open and vast. It is receptive to everything, but holds on to nothing.

ATTACHMENT TO VIEWS

We also become quite attached to our opinions and views about things, attached to being right. It's instructive to distinguish between what we really know and what is simply an opinion. There are many examples of this confusion in our lives, but for me one story stands out as a turning point of understanding.

In the late 1960s and early 1970s I spent most of seven years in India, immersing myself in the practice and study of Theravada Buddhist teachings. A key figure in these teachings was Sariputra, the chief disciple of the Buddha. He was fully enlightened and second only to the Buddha in his wisdom. After my time in India, I returned to America and began teaching during the summer sessions at Naropa Institute in Boulder, Colorado. During one of those sessions I saw a notice for a talk to be given by Dudjom Rinpoche, the head of the Nyingma school of Tibetan Buddhism and a most highly respected and revered lama. One small part of the poster said Rinpoche was considered the incarnation of Sariputra. When I saw this my mind stopped. How could that be? Sariputra was fully enlightened, and, based on my studies in Bodh Gaya, I was sure he was no longer reborn. Yet Dudjom Rinpoche himself was considered a great and enlightened being. As I struggled with this dilemma, I had a certain epiphany. I realized I truly had no idea whether or not Rinpoche was the incarnation of Sariputra, and since I didn't know, I really had no need to have an opinion about it. It was an amazing and immediate relief, and I understood the tremendous burden of being attached to opinions and views that were not part of my direct experience. This doesn't mean we might not have such views, only that the strong attachment to them may be a burden we no longer wish to carry.

This brings us back to one of the fundamental disagreements between different Buddhist traditions. Was there one Turning of the Wheel of Dharma, or two, or three? If we weren't there for them, or don't remember if we were, our opinions about it will simply reflect the biases of what we have read and heard. Rather than taking a stand or holding fast to a position we don't have direct experience of, it may be wiser to reframe the debate. Instead of "Who's right?" the question becomes "What can I learn from this teaching? Can it help me free the mind from clinging?" When we ask these questions, then all the teachings—even opposing ones—can become skillful means for liberation. We are no longer sidetracked into attachment to views.

Besides not being attached to things we really don't know, it may also be wise to keep an open mind even about what we think we do know. Do we cling to what we know, closing off to other viewpoints, other possibilities? It's very easy to develop feelings of pride about knowledge or even insight, and when we cling to knowledge and insight, the seeds of strong sectarian conflicts are planted. Bankei, a seventeenth-century Japanese Zen master, expressed this well in a basic instruction, "Don't side with yourself."

Clinging to views is subtler than our attachments to sense pleasures, which, though they run deep, are not difficult to notice. But the views and opinions we hold are often difficult to see, even as they determine how we perceive the world and understand our spiritual path. It is sadly ironic when attachment to religious or sectarian beliefs becomes the cause of suffering. And we have seen this tragedy repeat many times throughout history, even to the present day. This is as true in Buddhism as anywhere else, and in some of his earliest teachings the Buddha warned against this tendency to exalt our own view of truth and disparage that of others.

A theme running through parts of the *Sutta Nipata* is how attachment to any view at all becomes both the source of contentious dispute and an obstacle to liberation. These two points are worth distinguishing. It is one thing to refrain from attachment to views as a way of avoiding endless arguments and thus abide more calmly amidst the opinions of the world; it is another to realize that the attachment itself, to any view, is a contraction of the mind, a bond, a fetter. Nonclinging to views is a doorway to One Dharma. According to the *Sutta Nipata*:

> "Excellent!" says the person immersed in views,
> Making out that his are the best in the world.
> "Inferior!" is everything other than this—
> He has clearly not risen above disputes.
>
> ———
>
> The experts call a knot (bond) that leaning
> on which one regards everything else to be lowly.

Not only do we contend with other traditions, we often become most strongly polemical about the views of those closest to us. Suzuki Roshi describes how this occurred in the time of Hui Neng, the Sixth Zen Ancestor. It seems several of Hui Neng's disciples had each compiled a version of the master's teaching and claimed that it alone was authentic. Roshi points out that there were many schools of Zen at that time, "and because they were involved in ideas of right and wrong teaching, or traditional and heretical teaching, they lost the main point of their practice." It is easy to become entangled in the net of views, especially when they are our own.

ATTACHMENT TO SELF

The deepest attachment that conditions our lives and understanding is the clinging to the concept of self. Although we may have some intellectual understanding of emptiness or even some direct realization of it, we continue to create a felt sense of self whenever we identify with any particular aspect of our experience. There are many examples of this. We see this clearly in the relationship we have to our bodies. This concept of body, which we usually hold and cherish, is often our first and most immediate response to the question, "Who am I?" We wake up in the morning, look in the mirror, see the reflection of the body, and think, "Yes, that's me." When we look deeper, though, we see that the body is not something in itself that we can call "me" or "mine."

Some years ago, this insight was brought home for me in a very graphic way. A friend of mine had a fibroid tumor removed through laser surgery, which is done by inserting a miniaturized video camera and laser through a very small incision. The surgeon then guides the laser beam by watching the video screen. As a parting gift, my friend received a video of the operation. Although she was not particularly interested in watching it, I became fascinated by this view of the body from the inside. I could see different organs and muscle tissue, the flow of blood, and the laser itself cutting away sections of the tumor. When we see the body in this way, we're not so likely to identify with the organs or blood as being self. Why, then, do we identify with it so strongly when it's all neatly packaged in skin?

And if we could look even more microscopically, we would see the body as cells, parts of cells, atoms, electrons, space—really, not much there. If all space were removed from the body, the matter that remained would be the size of a particle of dust. So what we're identifying with as body is really based on a very superficial perception of what in fact is there. Yet this identification goes very deep. It conditions the strong attachments we have to our own bodies and those of others. A consequence of this attachment is our fear of loss and fear of death.

When we pay close attention, we begin to get a different understanding of the body. As concentration deepens in both sitting and walking meditation, our sense of the form of the body begins to disappear. What remains is the experience of changing sensations, the body as an energy field. As an experiment you can try right now, press the palms of your hands together lightly, close your eyes, and notice what you are feeling. What sensations do you experience? In the sensations of pressure, warmth, tingling, and so on, what has happened to the notion "hand"? In just the same way, our notion of "body" is a concept that fixes a view of who and what we are. Seeing through the concept to the direct experience of what is happening helps free the mind from clinging to body as self, as "I."

We also create a sense of self when we identify with thoughts—the sense that *I'm* thinking, *I'm* planning, *I'm* judging—or when we identify with the stories we make up about our experience. They may be stories about our personal history or our spiritual journey. We also strengthen the sense of self when we get lost in thought projections about other people, sometimes people we don't even know. Standing in line at the supermarket, how many quick little judgments about people flit through the mind, not to speak of the major projections onto people that are close to us? On meditation retreats the "*vipassana* romance" and the "*vipassana* vendetta" are all too common occurrences. We may find ourselves fantasizing about getting to know someone, having an affair, getting married, having kids, all in a few moments of thought. Or we may have harsh judgments about people—we don't like anything at all about them—without ever having met them. We become lost in stories of attraction and aversion toward other people based on momentary identification with passing thoughts.

Thoughts are tremendously seductive. When they go unnoticed, they have compelling power; they become the dictators of the mind. Yet when they are noticed, we realize the only power thoughts have is the power we give them. We see that thoughts themselves are the thinker, that there's no "self" behind them to whom they're happening. In the light of awareness, thoughts often dissolve in the very moment of noticing. We see their essentially empty, transparent, insubstantial nature. Notice the difference in your own experience between being lost in thoughts and being aware of them.

The sense of self also arises strongly when we identify with various emotions, like anger, happiness, sadness, or joy. These are more amorphous experiences than thoughts and therefore harder to see clearly. Although thoughts may slip into the mind unnoticed, they still have a definite beginning and end. Emotions are more complex, involving feelings in the body, thoughts, or images, and different moods in the mind. When we're not mindful, it is easy to personalize emotions, taking them to be self. This happens so often in our lives: "I'm angry," "I'm happy," "I'm sad." And we solidify the sense of self even further when we go from "I'm angry" to "I'm an angry person." In that moment we have created not only a momentary sense of self, but also a more long-lived self-image. We have built a whole super-structure of self on top of what are really just ephemeral, chang-ing conditions.

It's possible to free ourselves from this energetic contraction into self when we see how emotions arise out of conditions and then again vanish in the clear open sky of awareness. One way of doing this is to focus on their contingent nature, being mindful of how often emotions are triggered and then fed by unnoticed thoughts and images. We may be going along in our lives, and then a fleeting thought or image arises in the mind that perhaps stirs a memory of some past event or an anticipation of some future one, which then can suddenly flood the mind with some strong emotion. It all happens very quickly. The more we see emotions arising out of combinations of conditions, the less we personalize them. This doesn't mean we don't feel them, but rather that we stay free in the transitory experience of whatever the emotion may be.

Some years ago I was on a rafting trip on the middle fork of the Salmon River in Idaho. It was my first time going through white-water rapids. Along with the group rafts, we also had a small, one-person inflatable kayak to play around in. One afternoon, as I was happily paddling down the river in the kayak, the guide shouted over to me, "Watch out for the hole!" I had no idea what he was talking about. I knew about holes in the ground, but had never heard of a "hole" in a river before. A few moments later I knew what it meant. A hole is formed when rushing water spills over a rock in a certain way creating a whirlpool. So there I was, in my little plastic kayak, going over the rock into the hole. The whirlpool quickly sucked me under the water, but a few moments later the buoyancy of my life vest pushed me back up to the surface. Again, the whirlpool pulled me under and again the vest helped me surface. Finally, the hole ejected me into the flow of the river current, and I floated downstream to where the rafts were waiting.

What does all this have to do with emotions? When we're not mindful, the strong force of emotions pulls us under, and their powerful energies toss us about. Mindfulness is like wearing the life vest. The emotions still come, but we are protected from drowning in them. We no longer take them to be "self" or "I," but rather experience them as part of the flowing current of life. There is a great sense of freedom when we don't identify so completely with every passing mind state and mood. The mystic poet Rumi wrote, "What I want is to leap out of this personality, and then sit apart from that leaping. I've lived too long where I can be reached."

On the subtlest level, we give birth to the sense of "I" when we identify with consciousness or awareness itself, thereby creating a sense of the witness or observer separate from experience. Even when we understand the transitory, selfless nature of the body, thoughts, and emotions, still we have a strong feeling that we're the one who knows all of these things. In meditation, one helpful way to cut through the identification as observer or witness is to language our experience in the passive voice, for example, to consider hearing as "sounds being known," or thinking as "thoughts being known." We can think of our experience of the body as "sensations being known." This way of expressing what is happening takes the "I" out of the picture. What remains is luminous awareness spontaneously knowing. No "I," no self there at all.

Rebirth

Sometimes people wonder whether the sense of self is there from the beginning of this life, whether we "come in" with it, or whether it develops through survival instincts and social conditioning. Or from another side, the question frequently arises, "If there's no self, who is it that gets reborn?" From the Buddhist perspective, most people take birth precisely because the *illusion* of self has not been dispelled. Someone once asked Trungpa Rinpoche, "What is it that's reborn?" He replied, "Your neurosis"—a modern casting of the teaching that we take birth again and again because of ignorance and craving. It is the ignorance of not understanding selflessness and the desire that comes from the self-centered reference point of our lives. In Buddhist psychology, ignorance and craving are the forces that condition "rebirth consciousness," the arising of consciousness at the moment of conception.

The well-known Tibetan paintings of the Wheel of Life depict the different realms of existence revolving around greed, hatred, and delusion, all held in the mouth of the Lord of Death. They also show a being on the path of liberation escaping from this wheel of death and rebirth. In all the classical traditions of Buddhism there is strong belief in rebirth from life to life and in the urgency of awakening from this dream of ignorance. Given the profound wisdom of the Buddha's message and the manifest wisdom of so many great beings, we should not too hastily dismiss this idea simply because it may be at present beyond the range of our current understanding. At the same time, there are ways of considering the possibilities of rebirth and freedom that make them accessible to us in the context of this life, here and now.

Notice how often we take "psychological rebirth" in different realms throughout the day. When we get lost in some pleasant fantasy, the "I" is born in a pleasure realm. If we are caught by some intense unfulfilled wanting, we take birth in a hungry-ghost realm. If we are lost in a sea of hatred, it is rebirth in a hell realm. And when the mind is suffused with love or compassion, we dwell in what the Buddha called the "Divine Abodes." The "I" is taking rebirth countless times a day, traversing the Wheel of Life. Whenever there is birth of "I" and "mine," born from grasping, there is suffering.

Sense pleasures, views and opinions, the notion of self— these are the arenas of grasping that seduce us again and again. As we go deeper in practice, nonclinging has increasingly far-reaching implications. It touches the depths of what binds and limits us, and brings us to the edge of what we are willing to let go of in our lives. The teaching "On the Faith Mind" by the Third Zen Ancestor, Seng-Ts'an, reminds us, "The Great Way is not difficult for those who have no preferences. When attachment and aversion are both gone, the Way is clear and undisguised." Having no preferences doesn't mean we retreat to a place of stoic endurance, hardening ourselves in the experience of pleasant or unpleasant feelings, or withdrawing to a place of nonfeeling. Rather, we become increasingly familiar with that open expanse of awareness that simply allows whatever is there to be there.

This teaching is simple to understand, but not easy to accomplish. Even when we have tasted the peace and openness of genuine emptiness, the habit patterns of conditioning are very strong. What is it like to be truly nonreactive to pleasant and unpleasant feelings? We can do a few little exercises as a way of practice. As you walk down a street enjoying a beautiful day, what happens if you suddenly come across something displeasing to the eye? Maybe it is a pile of refuse, or someone throwing an empty bottle out of their car window as they drive by, or a dead animal run over by a car, all squashed and bloody. What is the first reaction in the mind? Is there a pulling away, a dislike, an aversion to seeing what is ugly or upsetting? In the course of a day, notice when different sounds arise. Do we like some and dislike others? Do we live in the Great Way when we experience different tastes?

Some years ago I was teaching a retreat in St. Petersburg, Russia. When I had first gone there in 1989, there were still major food shortages and even gathering enough food for the retreat was difficult. This time, about seven years later, more food was available, and I was enjoying meals very reminiscent of the Russian-Jewish food my grandmother had prepared when I was a child: borscht and blintzes, stuffed cabbage and kasha. One morning, though, coming down for breakfast, all I found was a small plate of coleslaw. Nothing else. I watched my mind go through a little dance of disappointment and annoyance. "Why just coleslaw this morning? This isn't a breakfast."

As I observed the mind reacting to unfulfilled desire, a desire for certain tastes and textures I had hardly noticed until it went unfulfilled, I began to think of monks going on alms round, receiving with lovingkindness whatever was offered. I thought of people who had very little to eat and who would have been happy to have coleslaw, or anything else, for breakfast. In the light of these reflections, I settled back into the moment of just eating, just tasting, and the mind became peaceful again. This was a small incident, but it showed me once again the strong habitual pattern of desire for pleasant experience.

We can experiment with these exercises at all the sense doors, including the mind, noticing the pleasant and unpleasant experiences that arise during the day. And in the moment of noticing these feelings, also pay attention to the myriad reactions of mind. These reactions are often the contracting, self-referencing forces of the various unwholesome mind states. They are precisely what pull us out of the space of open, empty awareness.

Some Tibetan teachings make an interesting and paradoxical observation about this: when we're identified with the afflictive emotions (*kilesas* in Pali), they obscure the natural openness of mind, yet the greater the defilement, the stronger the awareness. What does this mean? When we're lost in the various *kilesas*, there is that contraction of heart into a sense of self and separation, colored by some particular emotional tone. It may be one of the traditional "five classes of hindrances": desire and lust, ill will, dullness and confusion, worry and agitation, different kinds of doubt. Or it may be many other varieties of feeling as well. The Abhidharma lists fourteen unwholesome mental factors that color all the unwholesome states of mind.

But the very intensity of these states also has the potential to awaken us from the dream—the greater the intensity, the louder the wake-up call. Suffering can remind us to investigate: "What's happening? How can I understand what's going on?" If we remember the skillful means of liberation—that nothing whatsoever is to be clung to as "I" or "mine"—the very intensity of the defilements can provoke us into seeing where the mind is fixated, where it is holding on. We can then let go into the open space of awareness, of nonattachment.

There is a useful distinction here between nonattachment and detachment. Nonattachment is simply not holding on, not grasping, whereas detachment implies a distancing from experience, a pulling away, a stance of some*one* who is being detached. Understanding this difference, in the very midst of suffering, we can make space around the hindrance, the afflictive emotion. We relax the heart from the contraction of self-reference, seeing the insubstantial nature of the hindrances themselves.

Doorways to Liberation

How can we accomplish this letting go, this awakening of the heart and mind? Different Buddhist traditions emphasize different skillful means for achieving freedom. Some methods cross the boundaries of tradition, and some are unique to particular ones, but they are all in the service of liberation through nonclinging.

One powerful practice of nonclinging is the *awareness of impermanence*, which was discussed earlier as a way of turning the mind toward the Dharma. Here it becomes the very practice of freedom itself. We can become aware of impermanence on every level, whether we observe clusters of galaxies through powerful telescopes or subatomic particles through the latest quantum experiments. Perhaps more relevant to our own power of observation is the obvious impermanence of our lives: the body inexorably aging, relationships changing, births and deaths of people we love and of people we have never met, the momentary arisings in the mind, and the endless falling away of all experience, like water over a waterfall. Reflect for a moment on the high point of your life, the most wonderful moment, or the low point, the most difficult time. Where are they now? We begin to see that all our experience is part of an endlessly passing show.

It's strange that when we look back at our lives, it becomes clear that all our experience, from years ago to even the last moment, is like a dream. Yet in looking ahead, we are seduced again and again by the dazzle of possibilities, whether it is consuming the next meal, a new job, the next vacation, or a fantastic new relationship, as if some new experience will finally fulfill all our longings. It's through seeing and remembering the truth of impermanence that we loosen the grip of attachment and clinging.

When pleasant feeling arises in our meditation or in the ordinary events of our lives, can we contemplate the impermanence of that feeling, so that we feel it without getting lost in it, not buying in to its illusory promise of life fulfillment? If we're interested in liberation, the Buddha offered very explicit advice:

> Whatever feelings arise—whether pleasant, unpleasant, or neutral—abide contemplating impermanence in those feelings, contemplate fading away, relinquishment, letting go of those feelings. Contemplating thus one does not cling to anything in this world. When not clinging, there is no agitation. When not agitated one personally attains Nibbana.

Meditation practice is the practice of seeing impermanence very directly and intimately. We pay attention to what arises in our experience and all of our different reactions to it. We also notice what happens to objects as they appear. Any object at any sense door reveals the truth of change. Sounds arise and disappear, sensations in the body keep changing, and one breath follows the next. And each of these experiences is itself not a single event. Each is a current or flow of even more minute changes.

At one time, Ananda, the Buddha's attendant and one of the most beloved monks, was recounting the many wonderful qualities of the Master. The Buddha (here referring to himself as the Tathagata, or as "One thus gone") said in reply:

> That being so, Ananda, remember this too as a wonderful and marvelous quality of the Tathagata. . . . For the Tathagata feelings are known as they arise, as they are present, as they disappear; perceptions are known as they arise, as they are present, as they disappear; thoughts are known as they arise, as they are present, as they disappear. Remember this too, Ananda, as a wonderful and marvelous quality of the Tathagata.

Because the truth of change is so ordinary, we can easily overlook the profound and immediate results of directly experiencing the changing nature of phenomena. In one startling statement the Buddha expressed the great liberating power of seeing impermanence: "It's better to live a single day seeing the momentary rise and fall of phenomena than to live a hundred years without seeing this." What does this tell us about what we ultimately value in life, about what we devote our energy to? Here again, the framework of the two truths—relative and ultimate—helps us integrate these insights that free the mind with compassionate engagement in the world. On the ultimate level, there's no one there; yet this very understanding of selflessness allows for the natural responsiveness of compassion toward our fellow living beings.

Understanding the truth of suffering becomes another gateway to nonclinging. The Buddha said repeatedly that he teaches just one thing, suffering and the end of suffering. And what constitutes this suffering? "In short," the Buddha taught, "suffering is the five clung-to aggregates." What are these aggregates the Buddha spoke of? Just as a car or house is a collection of parts, connected and related in particular ways, what we call "self," "person," "man," and "woman" is likewise a constellation of continuously changing elements. The Buddha grouped these elements into five "heaps," or aggregates (*khandha* in Pali): material elements, feelings, perceptions, mental formations, and consciousness. These five aggregates constitute a being. Whenever we identify with or cling to any of these arising appearances, there is a feeling of contraction, of limitation.

We also experience the truth of suffering in realizing the unreliability of conditioned phenomena. It is precisely because conditions keep changing that they are fundamentally unsatisfying, like trying to hold water in a butterfly net. Suffering arises when we try to hold on or look for satisfaction where it can't finally be found. We learn a great lesson when we see for ourselves the unreliability of experience and realize we can't count on things staying a certain way.

Some years ago I was teaching a retreat at the Vallecitos Mountain Refuge, a wilderness ranch in the mountains of New

Mexico dedicated to bringing contemplative values to the community of social and environmental activists. The day the retreat ended we all took a hike along the river, climbing up and down canyon walls, scrambling over boulders, and simply enjoying ourselves in the great beauty of nature. As we were returning to the lodge, I suddenly slipped on a wet rock and landed very hard, hyperextending my knee in the process.

Later that evening, as I was getting ready to give the closing dharma talk of the retreat, I had the passing thought, "I should give this talk sitting in a chair." But I ignored the intuition, and proceeded to sit cross-legged on my cushion for the next hour. By the end of the talk, I could barely stand: hyperextension and sitting cross-legged were not a good combination. Friends needed to carry me back to where I was staying. All that night, as I thought of my busy summer schedule and the inconvenience of not being able to get around very easily, I watched my mind go back and forth between two quite different mind states—self-recrimination for being careless on the hike and acceptance of how things were. Finally, a great liberating mantra arose in my mind, reminding me of the truth of things: *Anything can happen anytime*. Changing conditions are not a mistake. It's just how things are. We can use this mantra not only after the fact, but also as a daily practice of remembrance.

Sometimes people feel that recognizing the truth of suffering conditions a pessimistic outlook on life, that somehow it is life-denying. Actually, it is quite the reverse. By denying what is true, for example, the truth of impermanence, we live in a world of illusion and enchantment. Then when circumstances change in ways we don't like, we feel disappointed, angry, or bitter. The Buddha expressed the liberating power of seeing the unreliability of conditions: "All that is subject to arising is subject to cessation. Becoming disenchanted one becomes dispassionate. Through dispassion the mind is liberated."

It's telling that in English "disenchanted," "disillusioned," and "dispassionate" often have a negative connotation. But looking more closely at their meaning reveals their connection to freedom. Becoming disenchanted means breaking the spell of enchantment, waking up into a greater and fuller reality. This is the happy ending of so many great myths and fairy tales. Being disillusioned is not the same as being disappointed or discouraged. It is a reconnection with what is true, free of illusion. And "dispassionate" does not mean indifference or lack of vital energy for living. Rather, it is the mind of great openness and equanimity, free of grasping.

We also accomplish the goal of liberation through nonclinging by realizing the *selfless nature of all phenomena*. Although most spiritual traditions speak of the transitory nature of phenomena and of the suffering that exists in this world, the Buddha's emphasis on selflessness can be seen as the great liberating jewel of his teaching.

We realize selflessness when we directly and clearly see that there is no existing independent "thing" that the words "self" and "I" refer to. We have a surface recognition of certain physical, mental, and emotional events, a certain pattern of experience, and we designate it with a concept, "self." Further, we name this concept, for example, "Joseph," and then believe that this name, this idea of self, is some existing reference point behind all experience—a "someone" to whom everything is happening. But "Joseph" and "self" are just thought fabrications of our minds designating an appearance arising out of a mosaic of changing elements.

A rainbow is a good analogy. We go outside after a rainstorm and feel that moment of delight at the sight of a rainbow in the sky. Mostly, we simply enjoy the sight without investigating the real nature of what is happening. But when we look more deeply, it becomes clear that there is no "thing" called rainbow apart from the particular conditions of air and moisture and light.

Along certain coastlines there is a natural phenomenon called a blowhole. Blowholes are formed when lava flows to the ocean and creates a cave with a small hole at the top. The cave is open to the waves, and as the water rushes in, the enormous pressure of the surf against the back wall of the cave forces jets of water out of the hole in a powerful geyserlike spray.

Once, while visiting Maui in the Hawaiian Islands, a friend and I hiked to one of these blowholes on the North Shore. As the water shot up in the air, a rainbow appeared out of the play of water, air, and sunlight; and in the next moment the rainbow dissolved as the water particles in the spray fell away. A couple of minutes later, there was a new powerful eruption through the blowhole and a new momentary rainbow. At times if clouds were covering the sun when the water shot up, no rainbow occurred. In this ongoing grand display of the elements, the empty, insubstantial, conditional nature of the rainbow became clear. It is not something waiting backstage (or behind the clouds) to make an appearance; rather, it comes into being only when the right conditions are present. Likewise, for each one of us, what we call "self" or "me" is like that rainbow—an appearance, a display arising out of the various changing elements of mind and body interacting with one another.

But even when we realize the contingent nature of what we call "rainbow," we still use the word as a convenient designation. On seeing the beautiful arc of color in the sky, we probably wouldn't say to a friend, "I just saw light mixing with moisture in the air producing a spectrum of color." No, more likely we would say, "Hey, look at the beautiful rainbow." Concepts are useful. And knowing that "rainbow" is just a designation for an appearance doesn't change anything in our perception of it. The phenomenon remains exactly as it has always been. We simply are not misperceiving it to be something substantial and existing in itself. Understanding this, we don't go chasing after the pot of gold rumored to be at the end of it.

But because we don't understand "self" to be a concept, just like "rainbow," we often do go chasing the pot of gold at the end of this rainbow of self. We keep looking and hoping that this self will find satisfaction or completion or happiness, never understanding that the problem is in the very self that is seeking. The writer Wei Wu Wei wrote, "It's like a dog barking up a tree that isn't there."

Another, more classical metaphor assists in understanding that what we call "me" is only an image of changing elements coming together. It is the metaphor of a chariot, as the nun Vajira refers to below. In one of the Pali Suttas, there is a dialogue between this enlightened nun and Mara, the personification of ignorance and delusion. This exchange goes to the heart of our practice, the clarification of self and selflessness, suffering and freedom:

At one time in Savatthi, the nun Vajira, getting up in the morning, took her bowl and robe and entered Savatthi for alms. After eating and returning from the alms round, she went into the forest and sat under a tree for her daily meditation. Then Mara, the evil one, wanting to arouse fear, trembling and dread in the nun Vajira, and wanting her concentration to fall away, went and addressed her with a verse.

"By whom is this being created? Where is the maker of this being? How does this being arise? How does this being cease?"

Then this occurred to the nun Vajira: "Who could this be—human or otherworldly being—addressing me with a verse? This must be Mara, the evil one, wanting to arouse fear, trembling and dread in me, and wanting me to fall away from concentration." So the nun Vajira knew this was Mara and she addressed him back with a verse.

"Why talk on about a 'being,' Mara? Are you not just lost in wrong views? This is just a tangle of conditions. Here a being is not to be found. Just as the word 'chariot' designates an arrangement of parts, so where there are the aggregates, there occurs the concept 'being.' There is nothing but suffering arising; nothing but suffering which ceases."

Then Mara, the evil one, thought: this nun Vajira knows me. And depressed and suffering, he vanished from that very spot.

"Here a being is not to be found." This is the transforming realization of selflessness. Physical sensations, feelings, perceptions, mental formations, and consciousness are not self, because they are arising and passing away each moment. Nothing lasts long enough to be called self. There are times in meditation when as soon as we notice something it's gone, and sometimes even faster than that. No past, no future, no present.

Is the self, then, something other than these five aggregates? We see that we are not these five constituent elements and that we are not anything other than them either. There is nothing that can truly be called self, nothing to be clung to as "I" or "mine." The self or "I" is not something we have to get rid of, because it was never there in the first place. This is a radical transformation of understanding. To the degree that we glimpse the deep meaning of this, the notion of self or "I" no longer drives us so powerfully in our lives.

The question then arises whether the self exists as the combination of the aggregates. This is, in fact, how we commonly use the term: "self" designates the *appearance* of the aggregates as they exist in relationship to one another, much like the appearance of a person in a mosaic of colored tiles. "Self" is a useful conventional term and makes for ease of communication. The danger lies in taking this designation to be something real. When we create the notion of an existing "self" apart from the interplay of changing elements, we get attached to a concept that has no substantial reality. Then, when inevitable change happens, we suffer because of that attachment.

Another way we realize selflessness is through seeing that things are not amenable to our will. It becomes clear that "we" are not making things happen and that "we" are not really in control of how things turn out. It is all an empty-of-self unfolding process, empty phenomena rolling on. We cannot say with any hope of fulfillment, "Let my body never become ill; let it never age. Let me only have pleasant feelings, happy memories, and good mind states."

Every experience arises out of conditions, not because it has some independent self-existence or because it belongs to us in a way that we can command. If we wish something to happen, it's necessary to understand the conditions needed for it to arise. The thought, "May the water boil, may the water boil" will never produce the cup of tea. What is needed is raising the temperature of the water to the boiling point by some effective means. It is simply a question of understanding the natural law of cause and effect—the Dharma.

This meaning of selflessness has a paradoxical implication for our aspiration to awaken. One may think that since things are not amenable to our will, there's nothing we need, or even can, do to become enlightened. Indeed, there are some teachings today that say just that. The Buddha is saying something quite different:

> When a bhikkhu does not dwell devoted to development, even though such a wish as this might arise in him: "Oh, that my mind might be liberated from the taints by nonclinging," yet his mind is not liberated from the taints by nonclinging. For what reason? It should be said: because of nondevelopment. Because of not developing what? Because of not developing the four establishments of mindfulness, the four right strivings, the four bases for spiritual power, the five spiritual faculties, the five powers, the seven factors of enlightenment, the Noble eightfold path.

These various lists comprise the thirty-seven principles of awakening the Buddha declared to be the essence of his teachings.

Nonclinging itself arises out of conditions. We may have the highest aspirations in the world, but if the work is not done to create the conditions for those aspirations to be fulfilled, they don't happen. This is precisely in the understanding of what Buddhism calls "dependent arising." Everything arises from conditions, and in seeing this contingent arising, we see the emptiness of self in the process.

As an experiment, pay attention to those moments in your life in which it is obvious things are not conforming to your will. It may be some condition of your body, difficulties in a relationship, or being caught in rush-hour traffic. Whatever the circumstance, see how it is happening because of specific conditions in the moment and not because you want or don't want it to be a certain way. The more we perceive this understanding of selflessness directly—that things are not amenable to our will—there is a growing ability to let go, to relinquish the illusion that we are the ones in control, independent of the conditions necessary for something to arise. And the less our minds insist on being in control, the more clearly we can discern the necessary conditions for accomplishing our aims.

The Buddha gave very explicit advice regarding the practice of selflessness. In a discourse to his son, Rahula, the Buddha reminded him that every aspect of experience of the mind and body should be seen as it is with proper wisdom: "This is not mine, this I am not, this is not my self." We can apply these words as a powerful skillful means, both in formal meditation and throughout our lives, for the realization in that moment of the mind of no clinging. It becomes a mantra of liberation.

There is a certain critical juncture in our spiritual practice when there is simply no turning back. This occurs when we touch the empty, selfless ground of being. Even as habituated patterns in the mind play themselves out, the ground of emptiness has become the reference point for our lives. As Jocelyn King, a meditation teacher, said, "It's better to stand on the firm ground of emptiness than on the quicksand of somethingness." With this transforming insight, the gradual process of purification continues. As a rope that ties a boat to shore slowly disintegrates lying in the water, so too will all of the afflictive mind states such as greed, hatred, jealousy, envy, fear, and pride as we practice relaxing the heart, letting go of grasping, and opening to the mind of wisdom.

ELEVEN

NIRVANA

There is so much Everything
that Nothing is hidden quite nicely.

—WISLAWA SZYMBORSKA

IN OUR EXPLORATION OF ONE DHARMA, WE NOW COME TO
the most fundamental issue: What is the nature of the liberated
mind? Is it something already here that we need to recognize, or
does it have a transcendent nature quite apart from our ordinary
experience? Does it have any nature at all? One of the great moti-
vating impulses behind *One Dharma* came from my hearing
accomplished masters from different traditions talk about liberation in very different ways, each with descriptions that were verified in their own experience. It was a relief to finally realize that
there are different perspectives even on ultimate reality, depending on our own particular relative conditioning, and that there is a
way of holding these opposing views in a context of greater unity.

"Nirvana" has already entered our popular culture—I have
eaten in restaurants named Nirvana, listened to the music of the
group Nirvana, and seen a United Airlines banner headline on
Yahoo that read, "Daily Departures to Nirvana. Buy Now!"

Although it would be easy, and perhaps even appropriate, to decry the degradation of its meaning, the fact that "Nirvana" has entered our cultural lexicon suggests, at least on some level, an acknowledgment of its ultimate significance.

In India, the term *Nibbana* also has a popular usage, although it is somewhat more aligned with its actual meaning. (In this chapter *Nirvana* and *Nibbana* are used interchangeably, depending on the context of the tradition.) Ajahn Buddhadasa, a well-known Thai master of the last century, said that when village people in India were cooking rice and waiting for it to cool, they might remark, "Wait a little for the rice to become *nibbana*." So here, *nibbana* means the cool state of mind, free from the fires of the defilements. As Ajahn Buddhadasa remarked, "The cooler the mind, the more Nibbana in that moment." We can notice for ourselves relative states of coolness in our own minds as we go through the day. Notice the difference between being caught up in a desire and the moment when the wanting comes to an end. Can you experience the coolness, the relief of being out of the grip of some craving, even when the desire was pleasurable? Or when there's pain in the body, notice the difference when there's some level of contraction through fear and aversion and when there's an openness of heart through courage and awareness. These examples point to the qualities of Nibbana—relief, release, peace.

Ajahn Buddhadasa spoke of how the coolness of Nibbana continuously nourishes and sustains our life because it puts out the mental fires of greed, anger, and delusion. It would be impossible to live if these fires raged all the time. Temporary Nibbana is the temporary absence of defilements. The supreme state of Nibbana is when all forces of the defilements are extinguished. It's helpful for us to see and experience this temporary Nibbana, because it inclines us to experience absolute reality, the Unconditioned, the "Ultimate Cool."

Nibbana is said to be ineffable and indescribable, unknowable by the conceptual mind, yet it is also described as the deathless, absolute peace, freedom, and so forth. It is Nibbana that the

Buddha declared to be the final goal of the spiritual journey: "This holy life . . . does not have gain, honor, and renown for its benefit, or the attainment of virtue for its benefit, or the attainment of concentration for its benefit, or knowledge and vision for its benefit. But it is this unshakable deliverance of mind that is the goal of this holy life, its heartwood and its end."

Although all Buddhist traditions agree that Nirvana is the cooling out of the afflictive emotions, there are some fundamental differences of view regarding the essential nature of this experience and the most direct way to get there. Does Nirvana, ultimate freedom, transcend awareness or is pure awareness itself freedom? Is Nirvana something we make an effort to attain, or is it the essential nature of our minds?

We will be considering aspects of these questions in four traditions: two in Theravada, one in Zen, and one in Tibetan. In order to understand the import of the various views, it is necessary to lay the foundation for the discussion with an explanation of the five aggregates of existence mentioned earlier.

THE FIVE AGGREGATES

The five aggregates are the raw material from which we form a sense of self. The first aggregate is composed of *all the material elements of the physical universe*. Everything we sense as being the body is part of this aggregate. Usually we stay on the surface level of perception and think of the body as composed of arms, legs, chest, head, or perhaps, if we have some knowledge of anatomy, as different systems of bones, organs, muscles, nerves, and so on.

Another way of understanding the body would be to directly feel the physical sensations: hardness, coolness, pressure, stiffness, vibration, heat, and so on. Notice there is no sensation called arm, leg, or lung. In meditation this becomes very clear. In both sitting and walking practice, the perception of form, the shape or image, of the body often disappears. At that time, only the experience of rapidly changing sensations remains. We begin to feel the body as an energy field. And sometimes even that disappears, and there is simply the experience of space. At first, people may be afraid of settling into this formlessness: "If there's no arm, how can I eat?" There's no cause for concern, however, since the level of form is always available to do what is appropriate. We don't give that up; we simply see the underlying reality as well. For example, we may know through microscopic observation that a chair is mostly empty space, yet we still use it functionally to sit on.

The other four aggregates are all mental phenomena. The second of the five is called *feeling*, which here does not mean emotion, but rather refers to the very specific qualities of pleasantness, unpleasantness, or neutrality in all experience. These feelings play a critical role in the process of our conditioning. Pleasant feelings habitually condition desire, unpleasant feelings aversion, and neutral feelings forgetfulness. The Buddha emphasized how mindfulness of these feelings was necessary to free ourselves from these conditioned responses. The third aggregate, *perception*, is the quality of recognition and memory. We recognize the distinguishing marks of each object, create a concept to describe it, and then store that concept in memory for future reference. It is through perception that the whole world of concepts comes into play. The fourth is *all the mental formations other than feeling and perception*, including volition, greed, anger, love, compassion, restlessness, concentration, mindfulness, and so on. (The Abhidharma, the Buddhist psychology, lists fifty of these mental qualities.) And the fifth aggregate is *consciousness*, the knowing faculty that arises in each moment of experience.

Consciousness, when used in this context of the five aggregates, arises out of conditions. For example, visual consciousness arises when there is the working organ of the eye, a visible object appearing before it, light, and attention. If any of these conditions are missing, then that moment of visual consciousness cannot arise. This description of consciousness as being dependent on conditions, which is found countless times in the Pali Suttas, is a critical piece in the puzzle of Nirvana.

The Buddha emphasized this contingent nature of consciousness in a response to a monk named Sati, who had the view that there was just one consciousness that went from life to life:

> "It is this same consciousness that runs and wanders through the round of rebirths."
>
> [The Buddha then asked Sati,] "What is that consciousness?"
>
> [Sati replied,] "It is that which speaks and feels and experiences here and there the result of good and bad actions."
>
> [In quite strong language the Buddha then said,] "Misguided man, to whom have you ever known me to teach the Dhamma in that way? Misguided man, in many discourses have I not stated consciousness to be dependently arisen, since without a condition there is no origination of consciousness?"

The Buddha was reaffirming the understanding that in each moment consciousness is arising dependent on conditions and then passing away. This is happening so fast that we do not generally recognize it during our daily lives; however, in meditation, as we refine our attention, it becomes clear.

From this particular viewpoint, then, there is no awareness or consciousness outside the play of these aggregates. Consciousness, awareness, and mindfulness are all part of the flow of conditioned phenomena, and Nirvana is something quite apart. Practicing with this understanding leads through various stages of purification to an experience of Nirvana that transcends awareness. This is a classical Theravada view, especially as it is taught in Burma. But as we will see, even within Theravada, there are other viewpoints as well.

STAGES OF PURIFICATION

In practicing insight meditation according to the Burmese tradition of Mahasi Sayadaw, we pay attention to each arising experience. As mindfulness develops, we go through various stages of purification, each one leading to the next. One Sutta in the Pali canon describes this progression as a journey made with chariots in relay: "By means of the first relay chariot I arrived at the second. . . . Then I dismounted from the first chariot and mounted the second . . . and by means of the second I arrived at the third . . . fourth . . . fifth . . . sixth . . . seventh." Each purification is accomplished for the sake of reaching the next, all the way to enlightenment.

Although the Sutta itself does not give detailed descriptions of the stages, they have been well elaborated both in the great Theravada commentary, *The Path of Purification*, and by different masters over the centuries. A brief explanation of these stages may be useful here, as it will provide a touchstone for considering aspects of meditative experiences in other traditions. It is important to remember, though, that each person's experience may vary from the orderly progression of these stages. Sometimes we seem to go backward or pass through particular insights so quickly we don't even notice them. Different stages can also be confused one with another, even by experienced teachers. And sometimes there are deep psychological and emotional openings that are not described in this particular model of development at all. As a general guide to the meditative process, this map can be extremely helpful. But we should not become attached to the idea that it will always be an exact reflection of how our experience unfolds.

The first stage is *purification of conduct*. This is the practice and refinement of *sila*, morality, which we have discussed at some length earlier. Most simply, it is the practice of the precepts and wholesome actions. Because morality is the basis of nonremorse, it makes possible the necessary stabilization of concentration, undistractedness, which is called *purification of mind*. When the mind is well concentrated and steady on the object of meditation, the hindrances don't have the opportunity to arise. Concentration is like a fence that keeps out unwanted intruders; the intruders are still there, but they can't get in. Because concentration purifies the mind, temporarily, of the hindrances and obstructions, we are able to see more clearly, and so it becomes the basis for the growth of wisdom.

When the mind is settled and composed for some sustained periods of time, continued mindfulness and investigation lead to the next stage, called *purification of view*. This is a turning point on our path, because it is the first experiential understanding of *anatta*, "selflessness." We experience each moment as the paired progression of consciousness and its object, understanding that there is no one lurking behind this process *to whom* it is happening. At this time in practice, we see very clearly that everything we are calling "self" or "I" is simply the interplay of mental and physical phenomena, the five aggregates. Although this insight into selflessness is not yet complete and there are still many places where we identify with various thoughts and feelings, again creating the sense of self, still this stage of insight is a radical departure from our usual way of perceiving the world and ourselves.

As we strengthen this perspective and understanding of selflessness, we perceive directly that all of these aggregates arise out of appropriate conditions and see by inference that in the past and future the same law of causality applies—everything occurs due to conditions. When this is understood, doubt about how things happen in the three times (past, present, and future) is abandoned. This stage is called *purification by overcoming doubt*.

In the next stage, *purification by knowledge and vision of what is the path and what is not the path*, we come to a critical place of understanding. As our experience in meditation deepens, we begin to see with extraordinary clarity the momentary rise and fall of all phenomena. The mind has become like a shining piece of crystal, and the beginning and ending of each object is very distinct. We have broken through to a different level of perception, more microscopic in its focus, and we feel great joy, elation, and wonder at the clear, radiant mind effortlessly noticing the arising and passing of experience. It is easy now to meditate for long periods of time without pain or discomfort. At this stage, distant memories may arise in the mind and, for some people, even images or recollections of past lives. Everything we have practiced so hard for is now happening with ease.

This level of insight is called the forerunner of Nibbana. It is like a person standing with his or her arm raised in the air. Sooner or later, it will fall to its natural position. In the same way, once we have the experience of arising and passing away, realization comes in the natural course of our unfolding practice. (Of course, it may be days, weeks, months, or even many years, depending on our effort and our previous development.) This is the insight the Buddha referred to when he said, "It is better to live a single day seeing the rise and fall of phenomena, than to live a hundred years without seeing it."

But as this stage matures, we understand that these very wholesome states of mind—rapture, calm, clarity, and concentration—are now "corruptions of insight." They are called this not because they have suddenly become unwholesome, but because it is easy to become attached to them, feel pride in our accomplishments, and think that we have already arrived at the goal. Only through continued application of mindfulness to these states themselves do we see that they too are impermanent, ultimately unsatisfying, and nonself.

Impermanent, ultimately unsatisfying, and empty of self—these are the three characteristics of existence the Buddha pointed out so often. We see that the more ecstatic states of mind are, in fact, not the path that leads to liberation. So we understand what is the path and what is not. The importance of this discernment is highlighted in all the Buddhist traditions. For example, in the Tibetan Dzogchen teachings, great care is taken to not confuse the conditioned states of bliss, clarity, and nonthought with the experience of realizing the unconditioned Nature of Mind.

The next stage is *purification by knowledge and vision of the way.* Here the meditation progresses through a series of what are called "insight knowledges"—distinct experiences in practice that reveal more and more clearly the three characteristics of existence. One of these "insight knowledges" is the knowledge of dissolution, where the mind inclines toward experiencing the endings of things, so that each pair of consciousness and its object is felt as continually dissolving. There is nothing to hold on to; there is no place to take a stand. It is as if we are on the shifting sands of a very steep slope. Sometimes this perception of dissolution becomes so strong that we may see things disappearing right in front of us. Our perception is so refined at this time that the very process of seeing is experienced as a flow of change. It is a time in our meditation practice of great insecurity because there is nothing substantial to hold on to. It seems as if we have lost all ability to meditate—objects don't seem to stay around long enough for us to be mindful of them, and so we think our mindfulness has fled. At this time, support and encouragement from a teacher are very helpful, reminding us that even these difficult experiences are part of the path.

Following this is a period of fear, misery, and disgust, because we are seeing very directly and intimately the utter unreliability of conditioned phenomena. Nothing can be counted on to provide ultimate happiness or security. This is called the "rolling up the mat" stage, because at this point meditators typically want to stop their practice, roll up their mat, and go home. This period of practice has many parallels with what St. John of the Cross called the "dark night of the soul."

As the meditation continues to mature through successive insights, we finally come to a stage of equanimity, where the mind finds a perfect balance and rest in the midst of changing phenomena. At this time, there are no cravings or yearnings, even for the next breath or the next moment of experience. We are not choosing pleasant experiences over unpleasant ones. The mind is abiding in a very refined and effortless state of openness and ease. This is a happiness that far exceeds anything we have known before. It is as if we have been crossing a dry and barren desert and suddenly find ourselves in a lush and fertile oasis. At this point, the practice simply goes on by itself.

STAGES OF ENLIGHTENMENT

As the mind settles into this perfect balance of no wanting and no resistance, the flow of consciousness conditioned by changing objects can suddenly stop. In that moment the mind opens to, realizes, alights upon Nibbana, the Unconditioned, the Unborn. This is the last stage in the chariot relay, *purification by knowledge and vision*—it is here that our meditation practice has been leading, for in the experience of Nibbana suffering has ended.

The Buddha described the experience of the Unconditioned in this way:

> There is, monks, that sphere wherein there is neither earth nor water, nor fire, nor air . . . wherein there is neither this world nor a world beyond, nor moon and sun. There, monks, I declare, is no coming, no going, no stopping, no passing away, no arising. It is not established, it continues not, it has no object. This, indeed, is the end of suffering.

A story in the Suttas elaborates this further. Sariputta, the chief disciple of the Buddha, was addressing a group of *bhikkhus* saying, "Oh, the bliss of Nibbana." One of the *bhikkhus* then asked, "If there is nothing felt in Nibbana how can it be blissful?" Sariputta responded, "My friend, it is precisely because there is nothing felt that it is blissful." In this light we understand Nibbana, the Unconditioned, as putting down the burden of ceaselessly changing phenomena.

In this model of spiritual development, the moments of realizing Nibbana are called "path" and "fruition" (*magga-phala* in Pali). The path moment of realization is likened to a sudden flash of lightning that illuminates the sky and has the power to completely uproot particular defilements from the mind so that they don't arise again. This uprooting happens in successive stages, called the four stages of enlightenment. The power of the first path moment bestows unending blessings, because it has cut through the view of self that has kept us so long confined. It is the moment of becoming "a noble one," someone destined for complete awakening.

Although we may read about these stages of insight and the descriptions of Nibbana as classical texts describing the path of liberation, for many people walking on this path of practice, experiences actually unfold in this way, albeit with different variations. So it is not merely a theoretical construct; it is one description of how things happen.

THE MIND RELEASED

Masters from the Thai forest tradition describe the experience of Nibbana from quite another perspective. This tradition flowered in the late 1800s, when Ajahn Sao and Ajahn Mun, two monks who became renowned for their ascetic discipline and their extraordinary meditative attainments, settled in the forests of northeastern Thailand. Their disciples have continued the tradition up until the present day, and some of these teachers have described their own personal experience of the awakened heart/mind. Their understanding has strong resonance with Tibetan and Zen teachings as well.

Ajahn Maha Bua, one of these great Thai forest monks, speaks of the conventional mind and the mind released. The conventional mind is ruled by the tides of proliferating thoughts that are conditioned by ignorance and craving—that is, our usual mind. When these defilements are uprooted through mind-fulness and wisdom, then the true mind, or the mind released, appears to its full extent. Ajahn Maha Bua describes this true mind as simple awareness, utterly pure. This awareness has no center or reference point of self; it cannot be located in any particular spot. It is unsupported, unconditioned, unconstructed.

The five aggregates of experience still function, but they do not in any way affect the mind released. The nature of this mind, this pure awareness, is ultimate ease, the highest peace. Unlike our usual experience, this ease is not simply a peaceful feeling of the mind or pleasant sensations of the body. It is the ease of emptiness, the absence of all defilements. He goes on to say:

> Nibbana is constant. The ultimate ease is constant. They are one and the same. The Buddha says Nibbana is constant, the ultimate ease is constant, the ultimate void is constant. They are all the same thing—but the void of Nibbana lies beyond convention. It's not void in the way the world supposes it to be.

But great care is needed in our practice. We can mistake wonderful and subtle states of mind for the mind released. Ajahn Maha Bua writes:

> Once when I went to practice at Wat Do Dhammachedi, the problem of unawareness [ignorance] had me bewildered for quite some time. At that stage the mind was so radiant that I came to marvel at its radiance. Everything of every sort which could make me marvel seemed to have gathered there in the mind, to the point where I began to marvel at myself, "Why is it that my mind is so marvelous?" Looking at the body, I couldn't see it at all. It was all space—empty. The mind was radiant in full force.
>
> But luckily, as soon as I began to marvel at myself to the point of exclaiming deludedly in the heart without being conscious of it . . . "Why has my mind come so far?"—at that moment, a statement of Dhamma spontaneously arose. This too I hadn't anticipated. It suddenly appeared, as if someone were speaking in the heart, although there was no one there speaking. It simply appeared as a statement: *"If there is a point or a center of the knower anywhere, that is an agent of birth."* That's what it said.

This is the critical point: as long as there is any identification with anything, any sense of the "knower," the one knowing, then we are still bound by the conventional, conditioned mind. Through mindfulness and wisdom we keep deconstructing the sense of self until the pure mind is realized and only the ultimate ease remains.

But how can we understand this teaching about pure awareness in relation to the Buddha's exhortation to Sati that all consciousness is conditioned? This is one of the sticking points between the Burmese and Thai traditions. Two understandings of Nibbana found in Theravada teachings can provide a useful framework for holding each of these descriptions as different aspects of One Dharma. The first is *the experience of Nibbana in which all the aggregates cease* (*khandha nibbana* in Pali). There is no arising object to be experienced. It is the cessation of becoming. Imagine yourself in a kitchen where the refrigerator is humming in the background. Probably you won't even notice it. But the moment the hum stops, you suddenly feel a sense of relief, a sense of peace. In this analogy, all our conditioned experiences through the five senses and the mind are like the refrigerator hum. We don't fully realize the stress of the flow of phenomena until the moment it ends. It is the great ease of putting down a burden we hadn't realized we were carrying.

But even this experience of cessation is described in different ways. In the first, awareness itself is part of the hum and Nibbana is experienced as a gap in the flow of all sensory experience (mind included). For a moment, everything stops. Awareness and feeling cease. It is the experience of nonoccurrence, of zero. Sometimes the analogy of deep sleep is used to explain this "unknowing." When we are in deep sleep we do not know anything, yet when we awaken, somehow we "know" we have slept well and deeply. We feel rested and refreshed from the experience.

In the second, there is an awareness *of* Nibbana, an awareness of the cessation of all conditioned phenomena. Bhikkhu Nanan128nanda writes: "Here, then, is a consciousness of the very cessation of consciousness. . . . Instead of a consciousness of objects, here we have a consciousness without an object or support. Whereas, under normal circumstances, consciousness 'mirrors' or manifests something, in this concentration it is 'nonmanifestative.'"

Once the Venerable Ananda approached the Venerable Sariputta and asked:

"Can it be, friend Sariputta, that a monk attains to such a concentration of mind that in earth he is not percipient of earth, nor in water is he percipient of water, nor in fire . . . air . . . nor is he percipient of this world or a world beyond—but yet he is percipient?"

"Yes, friend Ananda, there can be such a concentration of mind. . . . Once, friend Ananda, I lived here in Savatthi, in the Dark Forest. There I attained to such a concentration of mind that in earth I was not percipient of earth . . . nor was I percipient of this world or a world beyond—and yet I was percipient. . . . On that occasion, friend, I perceived that Nibbana is the cessation of becoming."

Thanissaro Bhikkhu, a contemporary American Theravada monk, scholar, and meditation teacher, writes, "A few texts discuss a separate type of consciousness that does not partake of any of the six senses or their objects. This type of consciousness is said to lie beyond the range of describable experience and so is not included under the five aggregates. In fact, it is equivalent to the Unfabricated [Nibbana] and forms the goal at the end of the path." And in the *Long Discourses* of the Buddha is found:

Consciousness without feature, without end, luminous all around: here water, earth, fire and wind have no footing. Here long and short, coarse and fine, fair and foul, name and form are, without remnant, brought to an end. From the cessation of [the activity of] consciousness, *each is here brought to an end.* (Translator's brackets.)

Although consciousness is not usually described this way in the Pali texts, with most references being to its conditioned, impermanent nature, many of the great masters of the Thai forest tradition use the language of the pure heart or pure mind to express the state of unconditioned freedom. They may be describing the experience of the second aspect of Nibbana, namely, *the cessation of defilements* (*kilesa nibbana* in Pali). Here, Nibbana is not some transcendental realm, but this very mind unobscured by the clouds of ignorance, what Ajahn Maha Bua called the true mind, or the mind released. It is the mind abiding free of defilements, the final cooling out of all the afflictive emotions. What remains is awareness, utterly pure.

A striking and vivid image, from a discourse to the nuns in the Pali Suttas, describes this state of release:

> "Sisters, suppose a skilled butcher or his apprentice were to kill a cow and carve it up with a sharp butcher's knife. Without damaging the inner mass of flesh and without damaging the outer hide, he would cut, sever, and carve away the inner tendons, sinews, and ligaments with the sharp butcher's knife. Then, having cut, severed, and carved all this away, he would remove the outer hide and cover the cow again with that same hide. Would he be speaking rightly if he were to say: 'This cow is joined to this hide just as it was before'?"
>
> "No, venerable sir . . . even though he covers the cow again with that same hide and says: 'This cow is joined to this hide just as it was before,' that cow would still be disjoined from that hide."

In this metaphor, the tendons, sinews, and ligaments refer to delight and lust for conditioned experience, and the sharp butcher's knife is the term for noble wisdom, cutting through those attachments. Just as the hide is now disjoined from the cow, so too when the mind is free of defilements, the five aggregates are no longer objects of clinging. The mind is no longer bound up with experience. It is the mind released.

What, then, are the defilements that obscure this purity and ease of mind? There are many lists of unskillful mental states, but they all derive from three basic roots: greed, hatred, and delusion. These states arise in our minds with different levels of intensity. Sometimes they are strong enough to motivate unwholesome bodily and verbal actions: tendencies of desire or anger, pride or fear that move us to act. Sometimes defilements occur just at the mental level and do not manifest through body and speech: all of the unwholesome thoughts and feelings that influence our mental state. Finally, there are defilements that are not arising in the moment, but remain as latent dispositions in the mind. Any of these can manifest whenever the right conditions are present.

In one of his discourses, the Buddha told the story of Mistress Vedehika, a woman renowned in the ancient city of Savatthi for being kind and gentle. But her maid, Kali, wondered whether her mistress was really free of anger. Perhaps she stayed in good humor only because Kali's work was so well done. The maid thought to test her mistress and began getting up later and later each day. At first, Vedehika was simply displeased, but as her maid's lazy behavior continued over many days, she became increasingly annoyed and angry. Finally she became so angry, she took a rolling pin and gave Kali a blow on the head. With blood flowing, Kali ran out to show the neighbors, and a bad report soon began to circulate throughout Savatthi about Mistress Vedehika being rough and merciless.

When I first read this Sutta, I had an unexpected response. Although not condoning the rolling-pin action, I felt some sympathetic resonance with Vedehika's situation. If we are counting on someone to fulfill a responsibility that is indeed hers, wouldn't any of us become annoyed if she consistently failed to do so—especially because of sleeping late! And not just once, but over many days. However, the Buddha is making quite another point here, and noticing my own reaction gave me pause for reflection.

On a deeper level, this story reminds us of the radical, uncompromising freedom of Nibbana, a freedom that is not dependent on conditions being favorable but remains untouched by the changing winds of circumstance. The difficulties we face in our lives become a truth-reflecting mirror of our minds. Do we get upset when things don't happen the way we would like them to? Or do we respond from a place of wisdom? When the Buddha speaks of freedom from defilements, he is not simply talking about being in a good mood. This deeper freedom comes through a profound inner shift of understanding where the sense of self-reference has been purified. Only when we uproot even the latent defilements can we truly taste what the Buddha called the unshakable deliverance of mind.

It is this third kind of defilement that has subtle and far-reaching consequences in our understanding of liberation. Although we may have moments of genuine realization, as long as these latent tendencies remain in the mind there is more work to do. This understanding is clearly expressed in the teachings of Chinul, one of the great founding masters of Korean Zen.

Sudden Awakening, Gradual Cultivation

Chinul framed his teaching in the context of "sudden awakening, gradual cultivation." This approach starts with awakening, yet recognizes the need for the gradual cultivation of that state.

What is sudden awakening? It is the recognition and direct experience of ultimate *bodhicitta*—the mind's empty, aware nature, which is always and already present. So from this perspective, it's not something we need to get or develop, but rather something we need to recognize and come back to.

A mantra that has been helpful to me at times as a skillful means for not clinging is, "It's already here." When I'm meditating and I feel my mind reaching out for something, wanting something, or waiting for a meditative state of greater peace, love, concentration, or emptiness, this mantra comes to mind,

"It's already here." This reminds me that the practice is not about wanting, but about letting go into the wisdom mind of nonclinging. It is understanding that clinging itself is "doing," and nonclinging is the natural state of ease. In this respect, nonclinging is both the means and the end, the practice and the result.

But Chinul didn't simply present this teaching of what we could call the ultimate level of understanding. He also emphasized the need to gradually cultivate that state of awakening. Here, "awakened" doesn't mean that we're fully enlightened—given the latent defilements that are still present—but rather the momentary recognition of empty awareness (or aware emptiness). Having a glimpse of it, or even many glimpses, is not enough. "But although we have awakened to original nature, beginningless habit energies are extremely difficult to remove suddenly. Hindrances are formidable and habits are deeply ingrained."

So Chinul teaches that we start with awakening, recognizing the fundamental empty nature of awareness, and then practice the gradual cultivation of that awakened state. In a wonderful book of his teachings, *Tracing Back the Radiance*, a student asks Chinul why gradual cultivation is necessary after one has awakened to the truth. The master replies:

> For innumerable *kalpas* [aeons] without beginning, up to the present time, ordinary men have passed between the five destinies, coming and going between birth and death. They obstinately cling to "self" and, over a long period of time, their natures have become thoroughly permeated by false thoughts, inverted views, ignorance and the habit-energies. Although, coming into this life, they may suddenly awaken to the fact that their self-nature is originally void and calm and no different from that of the Buddhas, these old habits are difficult to eliminate completely. Consequently, when they come into contact

with either favorable or adverse objects, then anger and happiness or propriety or impropriety blaze forth: their adventitious defilements are no different from before.

Chinul is emphasizing something here that is of crucial importance as the Dharma comes to the West. Teachers and students alike may indeed have authentic openings and moments of realization; however, for almost all it is really just the beginning. The habit patterns of desire and aversion, restlessness and conceit run very deep in the mind, and unless we continue to practice, these patterns continue to play themselves out in our lives. The great danger is in assuming that we are done with our journey, that we have reached the final goal, and thereby justify or ignore unskillful actions and states of mind that may still be happening. Chinul goes on to say:

So how could you neglect gradual cultivation simply because of one moment of awakening. After awakening, you must be constantly on your guard. If deluded thoughts suddenly appear, do not follow after them—reduce them and reduce them again until you reach the Unconditioned. Then and only then will your practice reach completion.

Nevertheless, although you must cultivate further, you have already awakened suddenly to the fact that deluded thoughts are originally void and the mind-nature is originally pure.

This last sentence completes the circle, reminding us that although our moment of awakening is not complete, it still transforms the way we continue our practice. Even as we practice gradual cultivation, using all the various skillful means and methods to develop concentration and insight, we are now proceeding from that deep understanding that the hindrances and defilements themselves are empty and without substance. We are no longer practicing from a place of thinking that the different states of mind are somehow solid and belonging to self. This is the union of the ultimate and relative levels: sudden awakening, gradual cultivation.

THE NATURAL GREAT PERFECTION

The Tibetan Dzogchen tradition also points very directly to the nature of the liberated mind, calling it the "Natural Great Perfection." According to Dzogchen teachings this nature is always and already present—it is the essence of the mind itself. Shabkar (1781–1851), the great Tibetan yogi, beautifully describes this essence: "The mind's nature is vivid as a flawless piece of crystal. Intrinsically empty, naturally radiant, ceaselessly responsive."

What does it mean to say *the Nature of Mind is intrinsically empty?* To many people, this may not sound very appealing. Perhaps they imagine a gray vacuity or a blank nothingness. "Emptiness" (*shunyata* in Sanskrit) in Buddhism has many subtle meanings, but perhaps it can be most simply understood as the absence of self-centeredness. We usually think of self-centeredness as a personality problem, something our friends might suggest we go to therapy for. But "self-centered" has a more fundamental meaning. Self-centeredness occurs when we create or hold a sense of self to be at the center of our lives, a reference point for all we think and sense and feel. The self-center is the idea or felt sense of someone behind all experience to whom it is happening.

Most of us live in the gravitational field of this self-center, circling around our hopes and fears, plans and worries, our work and relationships. Our lives seem to revolve around desire for ever new experiences, even as we see them continually changing. But through sustained wise attention, through the power of mindfulness and investigation, we begin to leave this familiar self-referential orbit. We begin to have glimpses of the zero center of emptiness, rather than the self-center of ego striving, and this becomes the new force of gravity in our lives. We may have intimations of this in our ordinary lives when we enter an effortless flow state, perhaps in music, art, or sports. Things seem to be going on without us—and are much better for it.

In the early Sutras, "emptiness" referred to this wisdom of understanding selflessness. Later Mahayana texts emphasized that even the particular elements, or building blocks, of experience are empty of any essence, of any self-nature. Everything arises contingently and interdependently; there is nothing substantial at the core of anything. Nothing has independent self-existence—teachings not dissimilar from those of modern physics.

The Tibetan Dzogchen tradition emphasizes another aspect of emptiness as well. This is the empty, spacelike nature of the mind. Padmasambhava, sometimes known as Guru Rinpoche, the renowned Indian adept who first brought Buddhism to Tibet in the eighth century, gave these "mind teachings" in a root Dzogchen text called *Self-Liberation Through Seeing with Naked Awareness:* "It is certain that the nature of the mind is empty and without any foundation whatsoever. Your own mind is insubstantial like the empty sky. You should look at your own mind to see whether it is like that or not." This practice is not the deconstruction of the sense of self, but rather a direct recognition of the mind's empty essence. When we look for the mind there is nothing to find.

Although the Nature of Mind can be likened to space, it is not actually space itself. Space is a physical phenomenon—it doesn't know anything; it has no consciousness, no cognizing faculty. Similarly, the spacelike quality of awareness does not mean the feeling of spaciousness with which it can easily be confused. A very experienced meditator once asked Tsoknyi Rinpoche, a Dzogchen teacher, whether the experience she had while meditating of vast spaciousness was indeed the empty essence of awareness. He replied that the Nature of Mind is better characterized as groundlessness rather than spaciousness.

Spaciousness is a conditioned state of mind often arising from balanced concentration. Sometimes our minds feel spacious, sometimes not. But groundlessness indicates that every arising phenomenon is simply empty, meaning that it is insubstantial, having no essential self-nature.

The natural radiance of mind is its innate wakefulness. It is the open, knowing nature of the mind itself—the inseparable unity of clarity, awareness, and emptiness. The Tibetan word for "radiance" also means "able to know." The nature of this awareness is the great mystery of our lives. When we look for it, there is nothing to find; it is like looking for open, empty space. Yet, at the same time, there is this innate knowing capacity in all sentient beings.

Robert Kaplan, a mathematician from Harvard University, wrote a book about the history of the number zero called *The Nothing That Is*. He writes, "If you look at zero you see nothing; but look through it and you will see the world." This is a good analogy for the open, spacelike quality of awareness. There is nothing there, yet it is not nothing. Some Tibetan teachers call it the "cognizing power of emptiness." Or as Buddhadasa Bhikkhu taught, "We should really call mind emptiness, but because of the awareness faculty we call it mind."

From the perspective of Dzogchen teachings, it is possible for us to look directly into the nature of our minds, to recognize the lucidly clear, unfabricated awareness that is uncreated and deathless. Padmasambhava gives simple instructions: "You should look at your own mind, observing it again and again. . . . However many names may be applied to it, even though they are well conceived and fancy sounding, with regard to its real meaning, it is just this immediate present awareness (and nothing else)."

Many Tibetan texts use the word "amazing" as an exclamation of wonder highlighting the ever present, although often obscured, truth of our own minds. In *Self-Liberation Through Seeing with Naked Awareness*, Padmasambhava says:

This self-originated primordial awareness has not been created by anything—amazing!

It does not experience birth nor does there exist a cause for its death—amazing!

Although it is evidently visible, yet there is no one there who sees it—amazing!

Although it has wandered throughout Samsara, it has come to no harm—amazing!

Even though it has seen Buddhahood itself, it has not come to any benefit from this—amazing!

Even though it exists in everyone everywhere, yet it has gone unrecognized—amazing!

Nevertheless, you hope to attain some other fruit than this elsewhere—amazing!

Even though it exists within yourself (and nowhere else), yet you seek for it elsewhere—amazing!

Awareness is the great wonder of our lives. But even as we begin to look at our minds and recognize this immediate present awareness, we need to notice if there is any subtle identification with it or if we have created any center point of observation. In the naked awareness of Dzogchen, there is nothing to find, nothing on which to take a stand.

The Nature of Mind is ceaselessly responsive. In the Tibetan tradition, a simple image of ice and water is used to describe the movement from delusion to awareness, from ignorance to wisdom. Ice is solid, frozen. It represents the mind contracted in identification with any arising experience—when it is identified with thoughts, opinions, feelings, sensations, or awareness itself—taking the experience to be self, to be "I." Water represents the *nature* of mind, the wisdom mind of awareness, unfrozen, and unfixated, where there is no holding or clinging to anything at all.

A great discovery in our spiritual lives is that water is nothing other than melted ice. So in this expression of Nirvana, freedom is not some other state, but rather this very same mind that had been frozen and fixated and is now unfrozen. Of course, great care is needed in distinguishing water and ice; sometimes what we think is free-flowing water turns out to be slush. We may feel as though we're abiding in a totally open, groundless space of mind, when in reality, there may be subtle attachments present, even to that state of openness itself. For this reason, Dzogchen teachings speak often of having confidence in one's experience, but continuing to clarify and refine one's view.

Lines from Wendell Berry's poem "Breaking" capture the importance of this clarifying process:

> Did I believe I had a clear mind?
> It was like the water of a river
> flowing shallow over the ice. And now
> that the rising water has broken
> the ice, I see that what I thought
> was the light is part of the dark.

In the open, unobstructed nature of awareness, there is great spontaneity and responsiveness to situations. It is like water flowing down a mountain, making its way to the ocean. Given the particulars of the topography, the water always finds the most direct way. The mind is not some inert vacuum, but is ceaselessly responsive to all arising experience. One expression of this responsiveness is a natural compassion—not compassion as a stance, but as the spontaneous expression of emptiness. The Dalai Lama is such a good example of this union of compassion and emptiness manifesting in the world: he laughs at himself and deeply cares for others.

In this fourth representation of the liberated mind, there is a shift from seeing Nirvana as being separate from the aggregates of experience to seeing it as one with them, with the explicit understanding that this union of emptiness and awareness is endowed with the heart of compassion: intrinsically empty, naturally radiant, ceaselessly responsive. The Dzogchen view is that all experiences are appearances at play in the vast expanse of empty awareness. They are the self-display of the ultimate. Buddhas are beings who realize this fully; ordinary sentient beings do not. Here, the path of practice is recognizing this union of emptiness and awareness endowed with compassion, and then stabilizing that recognition.

THE NIRVANA DEBATES

All these different expressions of Nirvana highlight a discussion that has been going on since the earliest days of Buddhism. What is the experiential, psychological dimension of Nirvana? Is it experienced as the ending of awareness, as something apart from the mind, or is it pure awareness itself? Is it an immanent reality, this very mind free of defilements, or is it a transcendent reality, something beyond the ordinary mind altogether? Even in the earliest teachings of the Buddha, there is much to support each of these views. And in the understanding of One Dharma, we see that they may well be different aspects of the same realization.

Most of us are familiar with the example of several blind men each touching a different part of an elephant and then describing the elephant based on the part they had touched. The same situation can happen in spiritual practice, even when our eyes can see and our minds have opened. The way we describe experience reflects many kinds of conditioning—the propensities of our minds, the practices we have done, the texts we have studied, and even the language we speak. Moreover, the limitations of language themselves force us to describe the truth in ways that can never fully capture its every dimension. Nirvana has been described as ultimate peace, the supreme silence, the end of suffering, complete freedom, the Unborn, absolute emptiness, the all-good, stainless beauty: same elephant, different words.

In *The Path of Purification* we find one example of how the different propensities of our minds can determine the particular way we experience Nirvana and the words we use to express it. According to this classic text, people's experience of Nirvana will be influenced by the doorway through which they enter: people who enter through the door of impermanence are strong in faith and resolution, and experience the Unconditioned as signless, meaning there is no sign there of impermanence. Those who enter through suffering are strong in concentration and tranquillity, and experience the Unconditioned as desireless. And those who enter through selflessness are strong in wisdom and experience the Unconditioned as void.

Within the Tibetan tradition, there has also been an ongoing debate about which of the three turnings of the Wheel of the Dharma represents the highest truth. It is a debate between those who give primacy to the teachings of emptiness in the second turning and those who see the teachings of intrinsic Buddha-Nature in the third turning as being more complete or ultimate. The subtleties of the arguments have been well explained in Reginald Ray's book *Indestructible Truth*. The point here is simply that even within one tradition, enlightened masters have different perspectives on ultimate reality, not to speak of the differences between traditions.

Another possible framework for understanding different descriptions of Nirvana is the Mahayana elaboration of the three bodies (*kayas* in Pali and Sanskrit) of the Buddha. These three *kayas* are classified in many ways. Most commonly, they refer to the Buddha's physical form, called the Nirmanakaya; his visionary, nonmaterial body in which he taught in other realms, the Sambhogakaya; and the body of ultimate truth, the Dharmakaya. This last is what the Buddha referred to when he said, "You can look at this physical form for a hundred years and not see the Buddha. Only those who see the Dharma see the Buddha."

Within the Dzogchen context of Mind Essence, though, these three bodies of the Buddha (in reverse order) refer to the aspects of mind nature mentioned earlier: intrinsically empty, naturally radiant, and ceaselessly responsive. These meanings may also shed light on the different views of Nirvana. Perhaps the path and fruition moments described as cessation of knowing are the direct realization of the empty, uncreated nature of Dharmakaya; that the simple and utterly pure awareness of mind beyond any defilement is the clear, cognizant nature of the Sambhogakaya. And when we speak of the Buddha after his enlightenment as "living" in Nirvana, all of this enlightened unobstructed activity is the Nirmanakaya.

As we consider all these views about Nirvana, we may find ourselves following our usual habit of mind, jumping in with judgments about each view, which ones we agree with, which ones we don't, setting one against the other. By making one view (our favorite) the highest, the others must be lower. But if we follow the Buddha's advice about letting go of attachment to all views and experience the freedom and openness of mind in that relinquishment, then, in the light of One Dharma, there is a way of seeing all the different perspectives as a mandala of skillful means, each contributing to our liberation. The description of the liberated mind may vary depending on what aspect is being emphasized and on our own particular conditioning. We experience the new moon and full moon quite differently, but it is the same moon hanging in the sky, changing only according to our relative perspective.

Do all these views about Nirvana have any real significance for us? Or are they of interest only to philosophers and to arhants and bodhisattvas far along the path? At different times in our lives and meditation practice we may get glimpses of something beyond our ordinary, conventional reality, touching a space that transforms our vision of who we are and what the world is. These intimations give passionate meaning to questions of ultimate truth, because although we may not always be living in that space, we understand it to be the source of everything we value.

TWELVE

THE SWORD OF WISDOM

The barn's burnt down.
Now I can see the moon.

—MASAHIDE

WE BEGAN THE JOURNEY OF ONE DHARMA WITH THE FIRST
steps of entering the path and the understanding of unwholesome and wholesome actions of body, speech, and mind. We discussed the development of love and compassion, manifesting
through the rare gem of *bodhicitta*. We explored the wisdom of
nonclinging, which leads to the highest goal, Nirvana. And
throughout, we have seen how teachings from different traditions can intertwine in harmonious, rather than divisive, ways.
Now we return to the questions raised in the Introduction to this
book. Is the path of One Dharma a melting-pot approach that is
simply making for a thin soup? Or is a synthesis of traditions
occurring that is vitalizing and strengthening our understanding?
The answer is, in fact, either of these, depending on how we
practice. One Dharma is like a sharp-edged sword: handled prop-
erly, it cuts through illusion and ignorance; handled improperly,
we hurt ourselves.

As we face the inevitable difficulties and challenges of working with our minds, the temptation will always be to look for some easier way, some other teacher or method. This misses a crucial point in practice: difficulties are part of the path. After some time of working with Sayadaw U Pandita, I began to appreciate the strength that comes from extending beyond the boundaries of comfort zones. Given my own deep-seated inclination toward ease and comfort, a mantra that in times of choice helped me remember the possibility of extending limits was "Choose the difficult."

Walking the path of awakening is like training in any discipline. For example, in recent years I have become a great mountain-biking enthusiast. Although I'm still a beginner, it has been instructive to watch how right effort applies to biking just as it does to meditation practice. When I began, there were trails on nearby hills that I simply could not ride up; even walking the hardest parts of the trail, I would still arrive at the top exhausted and panting from the effort, while some of my more experienced biking companions would be waiting there for me, lounging against the trees, quite at ease. At first, I would go up those trails only when I was riding with others, so I could be pulled along in the wake of their skill and stamina. But at a certain point I found myself riding alone and actually wanting to challenge myself— can I do this? The difficulty and exertion became part of the joy of riding. And over time, as I found myself getting stronger, my mind felt happier, the trails became easier, and I noticed myself on the lookout for steeper hills. These are the gifts of right effort.

Of course, for those with other temperaments or for ourselves at other times, if we are caught in obsessive striving and comparing, our challenge may be to relax and let go of self-judgment and arduous struggle. We each need to find what is onward leading, rather than what is simply habitual or agreeable.

Although we would all like awakening to happen quickly and be done with it, for most of us dharma practice takes tremendous patience and perseverance over many years. As the Dalai Lama writes:

Within a short time-span, it is impossible to change all our concepts or the entire attitude of our mind. It needs constant application. Speaking from my own small experience, from the age of about sixteen or seventeen, I began to make some serious effort to change and improve my outlook. Now at fifty-five, some thirty-nine years have gone by, several decades have passed, yet still the result is not satisfactory! We do have to struggle, and to work hard—and that is the reality.

You and I may have a different view of the Dalai Lama's progress, but the point is one that is made by all great dharma masters. We need to devote ourselves to training our minds and to learn thoroughly, and in some depth, whatever practice we undertake. This takes time. Even in the various schools suggesting we are already enlightened and that we simply need to recognize it, the task remains to accomplish that recognition and remember it in the midst of our everyday lives. This does not happen without the right kind of effort, whether it is called effort, remembering, or staying present.

HARMONIZING DIFFERENCES

As we continue our journey toward awakening with whatever practices (or nonpractices) we have undertaken, at a certain point of confidence in our understanding we may feel ready to explore different methods and traditions. The Buddha's teachings contain a wide array of skillful means, a vast treasury of wisdom. If we are well trained in one method, we can then integrate the teachings of various traditions into the One Dharma of liberation.

In harmonizing the differences in these traditions, it is helpful to have a template for understanding their different approaches to liberation. There are two basic styles to consider. They could be called the "building-from-below" and the "swooping-from-above" methods of practice. Building from below starts with the suffering we find ourselves in, learns how attachments are its fundamental cause, and practices letting go of those attachments through insight into the three characteristics. Swooping from above begins with a glimpse, or intuition, of the open, innate wakefulness of mind, free of any clinging—and then practices refining and stabilizing that recognition, without giving much attention to the nitty-gritty of experience.

Both of these approaches are well grounded in teachings of the Buddha that all the schools agree upon. In one famous passage, the Buddha described as beginningless our wandering through samsara: "I see no beginning to beings who, obstructed by ignorance and ensnared by craving, are hurrying and hastening through this round of rebirths." From this perspective, ignorance has been with us always, and the emphasis in practice is to recognize the suffering it causes and make the effort to purify it.

Another perspective understands the mind to be fundamentally pure. Although ignorance and the other defilements are seen as beginningless, they are also understood as not being intrinsic to the mind itself. The defilements arise out of conditions and pass away when the conditions are no longer present, like clouds forming and dissolving in the sky. If they were an intrinsic part of consciousness, then we could never be free. In one Pali Sutta, the Buddha spoke directly to this point:

> This mind, monks, is luminous, but is defiled by visiting (adventitious) defilements. That the uninstructed person does not understand as it is. Therefore, I declare, there is no mind-development for the uninstructed ordinary person.
>
> This mind, monks, is luminous, and it is released from visiting defilements. That the instructed noble disciple understands as it is. Therefore, I declare, there is mind-development for the instructed noble disciple.

It may well be that the approaches of the different traditions are simply highlighting one or the other of these two understandings: beginningless ignorance or essential purity. Those who focus on how deeply ignorance is conditioned will see the many kinds of suffering it causes in our lives and emphasize the effort needed to uproot that ignorance: how to take the next step on the path right before us—the pitfalls to avoid and the obstacles to overcome. Those schools that emphasize ignorance as not being intrinsic to the mind will focus on the recognition of the fundamentally pure, groundless, luminous nature of the mind itself. But both perspectives are true, and each one supports the other for our ultimate realization.

We need to be honest about where we are in our practice and understanding in order to see which approach would be most helpful at a particular time. If our minds are continually distracted, jumping from one thing to another, with little ability to rest anywhere, the injunction to rest in one's fundamentally pure nature may not have much meaning. When we are mired in suffering, unable to find that place of peace, methods that work directly with the fear, anger, or jealousy may prove more useful.

The Dalai Lama recounts how even Milarepa, one of the greatest Tibetan yogis, faced tremendous difficulties and needed arduous effort over many years to attain complete enlightenment. Although we all would like to have been a great yogi in a past life who now needs only the slightest nudge to move into the awakened state, for most of us this is probably not the case. The Dalai Lama writes, "We should not be pretentious and think we are more advanced and well prepared than in fact we are."

It may also be that people are caught in a lot of striving in their practice, struggling with the defilements and lost in a sea of self-judgment. At a certain point, the teachings on the essential purity of the mind—"It's already here"—could be just what are needed to relax the mind into a place of greater ease and freedom. This is not a question of using the teaching to simply make ourselves feel good psychologically, but rather of using it to experience directly, for ourselves, the empty, open nature of awareness. And even if it is only a glimpse of "sudden awakening," it can transform how we understand the difficulties that still arise.

Two ancient Greek myths capture the inherent dangers of each approach and provide some clues about how to avoid them. The first is the story of Icarus, who ignored his father's warnings and on wings fastened with wax flew too close to the sun. Swooping from above without proper preparation and guidance can end in a precipitous plunge to earth. For this reason, there is much emphasis in Dzogchen and Zen teachings that the introduction to the nature of mind, or teachings on sudden awakening, be given by a qualified master to a student who is ready and receptive.

The second myth is of Sisyphus, who was condemned by the gods to endlessly push a large boulder up a steep hill. Stephen Mitchell, in his book of poetry *Parables and Portraits*, describes this situation of suffering and also a way out:

> We tend to think of Sisyphus as a tragic hero, condemned by the gods to shoulder his rock sweatily up the mountain, and again up the mountain, forever.
>
> The truth is that Sisyphus is in love with the rock. He cherishes every roughness and every ounce of it. He talks to it, sings to it. It has become the mysterious Other. He even dreams of it as he sleepwalks upward. Life is unimaginable without it, looming always above him like a huge gray moon.
>
> He doesn't realize that at any moment he is permitted to step aside, let the rock hurtle to the bottom, and go home.
>
> Tragedy is the inertial force of the mind.

Sometimes, in building from below, we become fixated on the suffering we find ourselves in and on our efforts to be free. At those times, a teaching that points us to the freedom that is already inherent in us allows us to "step aside, let the rock hurtle to the bottom, and go home."

In the understanding of One Dharma, the highest teaching is not one view or another, but what actually works for each of us at any given time. If we understand the various points of view as different skillful means to liberate our minds, then we can actually use each of them to complement each other, rather than seeing them in opposition.

Most traditions, in fact, have a wide range of teachings, and an experienced teacher will be able to offer just the appropriate dharma teaching depending on the readiness of the student. For example, within the Pali canon, there are many examples of people becoming fully enlightened by hearing just a phrase or stanza from the Buddha—a direct pointing to the awakened state. Likewise, within the vast network of teachings in Zen and Dzogchen, there is much said about the fundamental teachings on impermanence, suffering, and selflessness.

How can we apply these different views to help us balance our own meditation practice? The swooping-from-above schools often encourage practitioners to abide in the Natural State, simply returning to it again and again. A potential danger here, and one that is pointed out by many masters in these traditions, is that we can easily confuse our normal state with the Natural State, mistaking "spaced-outness" for the open, spacelike awareness of the Great Perfection. If this is the case, some building-from-below, moment-to-moment mindfulness practice may be just the thing that is needed to cut through the drift of unnoticed distractions.

Another pitfall often experienced by those swooping down from above may be a reification of very subtle states of consciousness or an identification with awareness itself. Something is then needed to cut through these subtle fixations, to cut through any sense of awareness as being "me" or "mine." Something is needed to effect that radical transformation in which the belief in self-center is uprooted. Each school and tradition describes how this happens in its own terms, whether it is by realizing the empty nature of awareness itself or by realizing those path moments talked about earlier that go beyond awareness. In one way or another, though, we have to cut through our identification with anything at all.

Similarly, those building from below can become caught in their approach as well. In the traditions that see Nirvana as a transcendent state beyond the mind, practitioners often lose sight of the freedom that is already present in those moments when the mind is free of obscuring defilements. And practitioners in these schools sometimes miss seeing the essential transparency of the defilements themselves. We can become so caught up in a future goal or in a struggle with the demons of our minds (the hindrances, in one form or another) that we engage in warfare with them, rather than understanding them as being empty and insubstantial.

When we only emphasize our battle with ignorance, then we overlook the purity of mind that is always present, even if often obscured by our various attachments. As Chinul pointed out, "The Nature of Mind is unstained and originally whole and complete in itself." Even more encouraging, the spacelike nature of mind is unstainable. It's as if we were to throw some paint into the space of a room; the space itself cannot be sullied because there's no place for the paint to land. The groundless aware nature of the mind is likewise unstained and unstainable. So although ignorance may be conditioned from beginningless time, cutting through that ignorance is always possible.

When liberation from all suffering—both for others and ourselves—becomes the paramount issue, whether we swoop from above, build from below, or do some combination of the two, we find that the target remains the same. It is where the swoopers and the builders meet—in the heart-mind of awakening. The foundation of a nonsectarian Western Buddhism is the understanding that whatever the various descriptions of awakening or the path may be, the words themselves are not the experience. It is only in our own direct realization that transformation occurs. Freedom is the vital issue, not our ideas about it.

AN EMERGING TRADITION

Where is it all leading? We are in a crucible of transformation in which the diversity and depth of ancient Buddhist schools are meeting the openness and pragmatism of our contemporary Western culture. We face the challenge of preserving the rare and precious gift of Dharma passed down from the time of the Buddha, while at the same time cultivating a vital intercourse of East and West, ancient and modern. We are giving birth to a skillful form for our times.

The One Dharma of Western Buddhism emerges as a grand tapestry of teachings, weaving together from different traditions the methods of mindfulness, the motivation of compassion, and the liberating wisdom of nonclinging. These three pillars—mindfulness, compassion, and wisdom—are not Indian or Burmese, Japanese or Tibetan; they are qualities in our own minds. Multiple paths illuminate these qualities, and many practices enhance their growth. From the first moments of self-awareness to the full flowering of *bodhicitta*, teachings from different traditions inspire, instruct, and lead us to that place where we may truly be of benefit to all.

The practice of mindfulness has the potential to transform our society. We see the beginnings of this in the work of the mindfulness-based stress-reduction programs now spreading throughout the country. We see it in the mindfulness training of athletes and sports teams. We see it in programs offering contemplative mindfulness practices to groups of businesspeople, lawyers, journalists, environmental activists, scholars, and philanthropists. Most of all, we see it in the growing interest among people of all ages for periods of silent retreat. In the increased busyness and distractedness of our lives there is a strong need for the quiet transforming beauty of silence and awareness. It is from the depth of mindfulness practice, as well as its breadth, that realization happens and that awakening to wisdom becomes a treasured value of our society.

As we integrate mindfulness into the world, compassion increasingly becomes the expression of our spiritual path. It manifests in small, individual ways and also as larger trends in our culture. An evolving collaboration of practitioners who seek to actively engage with the suffering in the world has inspired what is called "engaged Buddhism." This movement draws strength both from the Buddhist teachings on *bodhicitta*, which remind us that practice is not for ourselves alone but for the welfare and happiness of all beings, and from the deep wellsprings of social action found within the Western Judeo-Christian tradition. Compassion and care for the world provide common ground in the many inter-religious dialogues now taking place. These exchanges are slowly breaking down barriers of isolation, suspicion, and sectarianism among practitioners of various schools and religions.

The essence of One Dharma is wisdom. We practice paying attention—to our bodies, our thoughts, our emotions, to awareness itself—and through a deepening concentration and stillness of mind, we gain insight into some basic truths. Wisdom sees the impermanent, ephemeral nature of experience and the fundamental unreliability of changing phenomena. Wisdom opens our minds to selflessness, the great liberating jewel of the Buddha's enlightenment, and to the clear recognition of the Nature of Mind: intrinsically empty, naturally radiant, ceaselessly responsive. Finally, wisdom brings the understanding that nonclinging is the essential unifying experience of freedom. We see that nonclinging is both a practice to cultivate and the nature of the awakened mind itself. As T. S. Eliot wrote toward the end of *The Four Quartets:*

> *A condition of complete simplicity*
> *(Costing not less than everything)*
> *And all shall be well and*
> *All manner of thing shall be well.*

Siddhartha Gautama set in motion the great Wheel of the Dharma more than twenty-five hundred years ago. It has rolled across continents and oceans, touching the lives of countless beings. Each culture has expressed the Dharma in its own language and idiom, emphasizing those methods that worked to free the mind from suffering. Now, as different traditions come together in the West, the unique opportunity arises to learn from them all and to practice the One Dharma of freedom.

ACKNOWLEDGMENTS

I AM EXTREMELY GRATEFUL TO THE MANY PEOPLE WHO helped bring *One Dharma* to completion. My heartfelt thanks to Harriet Barlow and the staff at Blue Mountain Center for creating an ideal retreat for artists and writers in the Adirondack Mountains of New York; to Diane Gedymin, whose great interest in the book was an impetus to proceed; to Hal Ross, who facilitated the initial meetings with Harper San Francisco and provided exemplary editing skills throughout the process of creating the manuscript—his enthusiasm has been contagious; to Eric McCord, who did the painstaking work of getting permissions for the various quotations; to Gyano Gibson for her unfailing, loving support throughout this endeavor; and to Reid Boates, my agent, whose good humor, steadfast encouragement, and many suggestions were tremendously helpful.

Many thanks also to my colleagues and friends who reviewed certain chapters and gave wise and incisive feedback. They helped fine-tune my understanding of One Dharma: Sarah Doering, Guy Armstrong, Rodney Smith, Sharda Rogell, Myoshin Kelley, Kate Wheeler, Thanissaro Bhikkhu, Lama Surya Das, Sam Harris, and Erik Schmidt. And to my Insight Meditation Society three-month-course teaching compatriots for the innumerable dharma discussions and debates that have kept us all on our toes: Sharon Salzberg, Carol Wilson, Michele McDonald Smith, Steven Smith, Kamala Masters, Steven Armstrong, Marcia Rose, Myoshin Kelley, and Guy Armstrong.

I'm grateful to Mu Soeng and Andrew Olendzki, directors and core faculty at the Barre Center for Buddhist Studies, for clarifying feedback, particularly on the historical material. They helped me to get it straight.

Particular thanks to Liz Perle, my editor at Harper San Francisco, whose fine eye for both structure and content improved the book immeasurably. Her suggestions were always right on the mark. Also, thank you to Terri Leonard and Calla Devlin of Harper San Francisco.

FOR FURTHER INFORMATION PLEASE CONTACT:

Insight Meditation Society
1230 Pleasant Street
Barre, Massachusetts 01005

www.dharma.org

*For more information about Joseph Goldstein's
other books and his teaching schedule, visit:*

www.onedharma.org

References

P. 14: "I would like to pass on one little bit of advice . . ." Dalai Lama, *Dzogchen: The Heart Essence of the Great Perfection* (Snow Lion Publications, 2000), p. 211.

P. 16: The Buddha's experiences during the three watches of the night. *Middle Length Sayings*, trans. Bhikkhu Nanamoli and Bhikkhu Bodhi (Wisdom Publications, 1995), Sutta 36.

P. 16: "I traveled through the rounds . . ." *Dhammapada* 153–54.

P. 18: The ten powers of a Buddha. *Middle Length Sayings*, Sutta 12.

P. 18: "Birth is destroyed . . ." *Middle Length Sayings*, introduction, p. 38.

P. 25: "I like to call the earliest layer . . ." Mu Soeng, *The Diamond Sutra* (Wisdom Publications, 2000), p. 14.

P. 31: "Why, being myself subject to birth . . ." *Middle Length Sayings*, Sutta 26.

P. 33: "Henry was never affected . . ." Walter Harding, *The Days of Henry Thoreau* (Princeton University Press, reprint edition, 1992).

P. 43: "Until one is committed . . ." Hallman and Mende, *The Rag and Bone Shop of the Heart* (Harper Collins, 1992): p. 235.

P. 44: "Be islands unto yourselves . . ." *Parinibbana Sutta* (Long Discourses, Sutta 16).

P. 47: "Keep your eye fixed . . ." René Daumal, *Mount Analogue* (King Penguin, 1986), p. 11.

P. 50: "I call on you, my teachers . . ." Trans. Steven Goodman and Bakka Tulku.

P. 51: "Mother Tereasa was asked . . ." Stephen L. Carter, *Civility* (Harper Perennial, 1999).

P. 54: "Just as, bhikkhus [monks] . . ." *Connected Discourses*, trans. Bhikkhu Bodhi (Wisdom Publications, 2000), vol. 1, p. 555.

P. 54: "It is 25 years . . ." *Songs of the Sisters* (Pali Text Society, 1991), vol. 2, p.11.

P. 65: "Bhikkhus, there are these five . . ." *Middle Length Sayings*, Sutta 21.

P. 70: "When a house is burning . . ." *Sutta Nipata*, trans. adapted from H. Saddhatissa (Curzon Press, 1985), chap. 3, vv. 591–93.

Pp. 76–77: The story of the Buddha Kassapa and the potter Ghatikara. *Middle Length Sayings*, Sutta 81.

P. 79: "I hope, Anuruddha [one of the monks] . . ." *Middle Length Sayings*, Sutta 31.

P. 81: "I, too, am firmly of the opinion . . ." Dalai Lama, in Joseph Goldstein, *Transforming the Mind, Healing the World* (Paulist Press, 1994), Foreword.

Pp. 82–83: "Monks, there are these four radiances . . ." *Gradual Sayings, Book of the Fours* (Pali Text Society, 1973), chap. 15.

Pp. 83–84: "The mind is restless . . ." *Dhammapada*, chap. 3, "The Mind."

Pp. 89–90: "Mindfulness is the root of Dharma . . ." Nyoshul Khenpo, *The Natural Great Perfection* (Snow Lion Publications, 1995), p. 123.

P. 90: "There is one thing we always need . . ." Tulku Urgyen Rinpoche, *As It Is* (Rangjung Yeshe, 2000), vol. 2, p.151.

P. 91: "Bhikkhus, if anyone should develop . . ." *Satipatthana Sutta, Middle Length Sayings*, Sutta 10.

P. 94: "If the heart wanders . . ." Francis of Sales, from *Perennial Philosophy* by Aldous Huxley (Harper Collins, 1990).

P. 95: "Once we recognize . . ." Dilgo Khyentse Rinpoche, Adapted from *Mind* (Editions Padmakara, 1990).

Pp. 99–100: "[Agassiz] intended, he said . . ." David McCullough, "The American Adventure of Louis Agassiz," *Audubon Magazine* (Jan. 1977): 9.

P. 104: "I have been hard at work . . ." Denis Saleh, Rattle Magazine (Winter 2000), p. 185.

P. 106: For a more detailed account of the passing of the Sixteenth Karmapa, see Reginald Ray, *Secret of the Vajra World* (Shambhala, 2001), pp. 465–80.

P. 110: "May all beings be happy . . ." *Metta Sutta, Sutta Nipata*, adapted from H. Saddhatissa, pp. 147–49.

P. 115: "When the Zen Master went out . . ." Ryuichi Abe and Peter Haskel, *Great Fool: Zen Master Ryokan* (University of Hawaii Press, 1996), p. 15.

P. 117: "Go forth, O Bhikkhus . . ." Vinaya 1, 19–90.

P. 119: "We should work for Buddhahood . . ." *The Diamond Sutra and the Sutra of Hui Neng* (Shambhala, 1969).

P. 121: "If a man comes to me asking . . ." Rinzai, *The Record of Zen Master Rinzai*, trans. Yoshio Miyakoshi (1990), p. 49.

P. 123: "except as we have loved . . ." Mary Oliver, *New and Selected Poems* (Beacon Press, 1992), p. 245.

Pp. 125–6: Story of Tendzin Choedrak. "Triumph over Torture," *Harvard Medical Alumni Journal* (Summer 1989).

P. 129: "For all those ailing . . ." Shantideva, *The Way of the Bodhisattva*, trans. Padmakara Translation Group (Shambhala, 1997), pp. 50–51.

P. 133: "When these five hindrances . . ." *Middle Length Sayings*, Sutta 39.

P. 134: "Nothing whatsoever is to be clung to . . ." Buddhadasa Bhikkhu, *Heartwood of the Bodhi Tree* (Wisdom Publications, 1994), p. 15 (a rendition of a phrase from the *Middle Length Sayings*, Sutta 37).

P. 137: "Don't side with yourself." Bankei, *The Unborn: The Life and Teachings of Zen Master Bankei*, trans. Norman Waddell (North Point Press, 1984).

P. 138: "The experts call a knot . . ." V. 798 of the *Sutta Nipata*, trans. Luis Gomez in "Proto-Madhyamika in the Pali Canon," *Philosophy East West*, 26:2, April 1976. p. 146.

P. 138: "'Excellent!' says the person . . ." Translated by Andrew Olendzki.

P. 138: "and because they were involved . . ." Shunryu Suzuki, *Branching Streams Flow in the Darkness* (University of California Press, 1999), p. 167.

P. 148: adapted from "Whatever feelings arise . . ." *Middle Length Sayings*, Sutta 37.

P. 148: "That being so, Ananda . . ." *Middle Length Sayings*, Sutta 123.

P. 150: adapted from "All that is subject . . ." *Middle Length Sayings*, Sutta 147.

P. 153: "At one time in Savatthi . . ." *The Connected Discourses of the Buddha*, chap. 5, sec. 10.

P. 156: "This is not mine . . ." *Middle Length Sayings*, Sutta 62.

P. 159: "This holy life . . ." *Middle Length Sayings*, Suttas 29, 30.

P. 161: "It is this same consciousness . . ." *Middle Length Sayings*, Sutta 38.

P. 162: "By means of the first relay chariot . . ." *Middle Length Sayings*, Sutta 24.

P. 166: "There is, monks, that sphere . . ." *Udana* ("The Inspired Sayings") 80, in Bhikkhu Nanananda, *Concept and Reality* (Buddhist Publication Society, 1991), p. 63.

P. 166: "Oh, the bliss of Nibbana . . . " *Gradual Sayings, Book of the Nines*, chapter IV, section 3.

P. 168: "*Nibbana* is constant . . ." "Once when I went to practice . . ." Ajahn Maha Bua, *Straight From the Heart* (Wat Pa Baan Taab, 1987), pp. 132–33, 142.

Pp. 169–70: "Here, then, is a consciousness . . ." Bhikkhu Nanananda, *The Magic of the Mind* (Buddhist Publication Society, 1994), p. 72.

P. 170: "Once the Venerable Ananda approached . . ." *Gradual Sayings of the Buddha, Book of the Elevens*, chapter I, section 8.

P. 170: "A few texts discuss . . ." Thanissaro Bhikkhu, *The Wings to Awakening* (Dhamma Dana Publications, 1996), p. 290.

P. 170: "Consciousness without feature . . ." *Long Discourses of the Buddha*, trans. Maurice Walshe (Wisdom Publications, 1987, 1995), Sutta 11.

P. 171: "Sisters, suppose a skilled butcher . . ." *Middle Length Sayings*, Sutta 146.

P. 172: Story of Mistress Vedehika. *Middle Length Sayings*, Sutta 21.

Pp. 174–75: "For innumerable *kalpas* [aeons] . . ." "So how could you neglect gradual cultivation . . ." Chinul, in Robert E. Buswell, Jr., *Tracing Back the Radiance: Chinul's Korean Way of Zen* (University of Hawaii Press, 1983), p. 106.

P. 177: "It is certain that the nature . . ." Padmasambhava, *Self-Liberation Through Seeing with Naked Awareness*, trans. John Reynolds (Station Hill Press, 1989), p. 14.

P. 178: "You should look at your own mind . . ." Padmasambhava, *Self-Liberation*, pp. 16, 22.

P. 179: "This self-originated primordial awareness . . ." Padmasambhava, *Self-Liberation*, p. 16.

P. 180: "Did I believe . . ." Wendell Berry, "Breaking," in *Selected Poems of Wendell Berry* (Counter Point Press), p. 82.

P. 182: Doorways to liberation. *The Path of Purification*, trans. Nanamoli (Buddhist Publication Society, 1979), p. 768.

P. 186: "Within a short time-span . . ." Dalai Lama, *Dzogchen: The Heart Essence of the Great Perfection* (Snow Lion Publications, 2000), p. 125.

P. 187: "This mind, monks, is luminous . . ." *Gradual Sayings of the Buddha*, vol. 1, chap. 10, quoted in Bhikkhu Nanananda, *The Magic of the Mind*, p. 83.

P. 189: "We tend to think of Sisyphus . . ." Stephen Mitchell, *Parables and Portraits* (Harper & Row, 1990), p. 48.

INDEX

Harding, Walter; *The Days of Henry Thoreau.* Copyright © 1983 by Princeton University Press. Reprinted by permission of Princeton University Press.

From *As It Is Vol. II*, Tulku Urgyen Rinpche, p.151, translated by Erik Pema Kunsang & Marcia Binder Schmidt, Rangjung Yeshe Publications, Boudhanath 2000.

From *The Diamond Sutra and Sutra of Hui-Neng*, translated by A.F. Price and Wong Mou-lam. Reprinted by arrangement with Shambhala Publications, Inc., Boston, www.shambhala.com

From *The Way of the Bodhisattva* by Shantideva. © 1997 by The Padmakara Translation Group. Reprinted by arrangement with Shambhala Publications, Inc., Boston, www.shambhala.com

From *The Natural Great Perfection*, by Nyoshul Khenpo Rinpoche and Lama Surya Das, with permission of Snow Lion Publications, Inc., Ithaca, NY.

From *Dzogchen: The Heart Essence of the Great Perfection*, by His Holiness the Dalai Lama, © 2000 The Terton Sogyal Trust, His Holiness the Dalai Lama, and Snow Lion Publications, Inc., Ithaca, NY.

From *Self-Liberation Through Seeing With Naked Awareness*, translated and © 1989 John Myrdhin Reynolds, with permission of Snow Lion Publications, Inc., Ithaca, NY.

From *Great Fool: Zen Master Ryokan*, by Ryuichi Abe and Peter Haskel, © 1996, with permission of University of Hawai'i Press.

From *Tracing Back the Radience: Chinul's Korean Way of Zen*, by Robert Buswell, used with permission of the author.

From *One Robe, One Bowl: The Zen Poetry of Ryokan*, translated by John Stevens, with permission of Weatherhill, Inc.

From *The Connected Discourses of the Buddha: A Translation of the Samyutta Nikaya* with permission of Wisdom Publications, 199 Elm St., Somerville MA 02144 U.S.A. Copyright © Bhikku Bodhi, 2000. www.wisdompubs.org

From *The Middle Length Discourses of the Buddha: A New Translation of the Majjhima Nikaya* with permission of Wisdom Publications, 199 Elm St., Somerville MA 02144 U.S.A. Copyright © Bhikku Bodhi, 1995. www.wisdompubs.org

From *The Diamond Sutra: Transforming the Way We Perceive the World* with permission of Wisdom Publications, 199 Elm St., Somerville MA 02144 U.S.A. Copyright © Mu Soeng, 2000. www.wisdompubs.org

From "My Crazy Tale" by H.H. The 12th Gyalwang Drokpa (Jigme Pema Wangchen). Copyright © 1991, 1995. English translation from the original Tibetan undertaken at the request of the author by Bhaka Tulku Pema Tenzin and Steven D. Goodman.

From *Straight from the Heart: Thirteen Talks on the Practice of Meditation*, translated from a Thai transcript of the answer to a question, by Ven: Acariya Maha Bua at Wat Pa bantad, Udorn thani, Thailand.

From the *Sutta Nipata*, translated by Luis Gomez in "Proto-Madhyamika in the Pali Canon," by permission of the translator.